Signed, Not Loved

A Collection of Poetry & Short Stories

Rachael Madori

ISBN: 979-8-9878123-3-4

Dedication

To my inner child,

my divorce lawyer and my English teacher, Mrs. Matlack.

Acknowledgment

A special thanks to AA.

"Honestly, it ain't nobody's business what's in my cup, what's in your cup, what's in their cup. It's your cup, drink it. "

Dwayne Michael Carter Jr. (Lil Wayne)

Contents

About the Author

Rachael Madori is a West Coast born but East Coast raised and based author. Rachael has been writing since she was 14 years old. Most of Madori's inspiration comes from a decade struggle with mental illness and addiction. Inspired by writers with raw and painful words, she's developed her own literary vibe; a sometimes uncomfortable but authentic writing style. As a public speaker and author, she addresses subjects such as suicide, active addiction, recovery and abuse to bring clarity and, with all intentions, hope in the suffering.

A Piece of Me

I am empty. I am full.
I am kind.
I am cruel.

I don't believe anyone who says they love me, because love shies from me in
a foreign city.

I am sorry that no one was there for you.
I am sorry that you were ripped up into someone new.

To kill me is to give me life
and everything wrong, to me, feels right.

I have been blind for decades and now I start to see.
You cannot possibly understand the death that lives inside of me.

Los Angeles, CA 1993-ish

The Frolic Room

I wonder, sometimes,

If people are already damned when they're born.

When I was in the womb - did everyone know?

"Fuck. She's really in for it."

I bet they saved the date.

March eight.

I was born in Los Angeles.

My mother met my father in a seedy bar

On Hollywood and Vine.

They were in love.

I think back then, and my mother was just in love

With a long-haired gangster

Who kept A .45 in the glove compartment

Next to the license and registration.

I think back then, and my father was just in love with a woman

And a Johnny Walker bottle he kept in the closet

Next to the skeletons.

No matter what their love was,   '

It sparked to make me.

She was already a single mother at twenty-three.

Just trying to live her best life.

Give everything my big sister would need.

My mom told him I was in her belly

Under a tree in Hollywood.

My dad drove me by that spot.

Decades later.

A Different man.

I don't think he was ready.

When he was under that tree.

Still, a lot of demons to fight.

Not a safe place for two angels to play.

He left for a couple of years.

But once some of the battles were fought,

There was room for us angels

To come to stay with him again.

I find it ironic

SIGNED, NOT LOVED

That all the demons he had been fighting

Saw what he made in my mom's belly.

They drooled.

Gums wet with Scotch.

Waiting for me too.

It's not his fault.

They were patient.

The funny thing is

The strength my dad has,

Knuckling demons,

From LA to New Jersey

Is in my DNA.

So when they came after me,

They had no clue who they were on the battlefield with.

They had no clue who my Chief was.

I am my father's daughter.

He may think that's a curse,

But I'm writing these words.

I've seen that tree.

RACHAEL MADORI

I've been at that bar where they first caught the eye

When she nudged her girlfriend sillily.

"I'm gonna marry that man."

A stranger.

He looks across the bar, stern.

"Come over here."

She listened.

I may have danced

With the younger friends of his demons.

They may still hang around.

Still whisper in my ear,

Bite at my ankles.

But from LA to Brooklyn,

I've fought them too.

So when we sit together now.

Him not old, but me much younger,

There is a heavy understanding

That the demons licked their lips

In that hospital room

When I was born.

SIGNED, NOT LOVED

Laughing at each other.

"We got another one, man!"

But I came out quiet.

My grandma was crying.

Afraid.

Because there were no cries of a baby,

So she says.

No sign of life.

I still came out

With big brown eyes,

Wide open.

Ready.

Uncle Ed

Uncle Ed would sit me on his lap.

On his porch in Compton.

We would eat Del Taco and laugh.

Just a little girl and her uncle.

Uncle Ed was a six-foot black man my dad had watch me.

But he was my uncle.

And I loved him.

And the Del Taco too.

Carteret, NJ 2001-ish

Dandelion Graffiti

When my mom brought me to the east coast from California when I was very young I met my dad in Carteret, New Jersey. Just shy of Staten Island. It was a very Eastern European populated area at the time. She would tell me that they would kind of stay in contact after I was born. One time she mailed him a photo and he wanted to see me. After he saw me in person, my big brown eyes and very full head of hair for such a young child, she says he fell in love. That he wanted us to be a family again and move in with him on the east coast. I don't know how that conversation really went down but my mom and dad make me feel very special every time they tell that story. Like I was the reason they finally got back together. I'm okay if that's not the truth. It's the little things, and maybe small fairytales, that get me through life.

I have some memory of California as a child. There is this point when your memories begin and before that there is nothing. For me, that started around the age of two. My first memory was what my mother's mother, my grandmother, refrigerator smelled like when I opened it for ice cream. I'll catch something similar to that smell even today and I'll remember that refrigerator in the hot desert of California when I was just trying to get some ice cream to put in a bowl and eat with my plastic spoon that was shaped like a plastic ice cream cone. I loved that spoon. It was so silly to me. Eating ice cream with a fake plastic ice cream cone. But mom had to say yes for me to have any. So I asked grandma because grandma always said yes.

I would run to the sliding glass door, the desert heat encapsulating me, I liked how it felt. I would climb our fence and steal peaches, maybe lemons? I can't remember what fruit. I would steal them from our neighbor's tree that was right next to our fence. We had a little hill that led up to the fence in the yard.

7

My big sister and I would play, laughing like little girls laugh, running down that hill that seemed so big even though it was probably very small.

One time she was in one of those red toy cars with the yellow top, where you had to use your legs to make it go. I screamed at her from the top of the hill. "Wait for me!" but she didn't wait. She just drove right on down that hill without me. Leaving me there. Alone. She didn't listen. It made me so mad. So mad when she drove to the bottom and got out, I fought her. We tumbled to the ground, two little girls grappling. I bit her stomach. Hard. Too hard. She cried and cried and I left a big terrible bruise on her. I don't know why I did it. I was just so angry she left me alone. She still remembers that, to this day. Twenty or so years later. We sit over a glass of wine and laugh.

"Why weren't we close growing up as teenagers?" I ask her once.

"Well maybe because you bit my stomach." She replied while laughing. We both laugh. It's our joke. But on the inside, I hurt a little bit. Because to this day, I still don't know why I was so angry at my big sister. Enough to really want to violently hurt her. Maybe it's because she didn't listen. Because she left me up there alone. But we were so little. Too little to know what alone was. But I felt it so deeply. Kind of like everything else I feel.

I remember the day we moved. I didn't know exactly why or what was going on. Just that we were no longer living with grandma in the hot desert. We were going somewhere very far away. My dad was there. Oh, I loved seeing him. His face made me so happy. A feeling I can barely explain. He was like this giant cool man who was so strong he could throw me in the air and still catch me like it was nothing! He must have been so strong.

I sat on the front lawn and saw the big moving truck on the road. I knew something was happening but I couldn't quite understand what. Eventually, we all got in the truck. Our golden retriever was in the middle. We were about to drive all the way to New Jersey. An adventure awaited us. Dad always took me on really cool adventures. Always. Even up until I was a grown-up. He always made time to have a Daughter Day and take me somewhere very fun, wherever I wanted. All three of my sisters got those. Just a special day we could explore the outside world, and see that everything wasn't as small as just school and our backyard. And if Daughter Day was during the summer we would take an adventure on his Harley Davidson. Those were the best ones. Daughter Days made up for the rest of the year when I would panic at the sound of the gravel driveway or stay up until the morning with my face pressed against the vent to hear every word. When I would get called a whore and my mom would never stand up for me. When I left a smudge on the bathroom mirror and would be told I didn't love my family because I couldn't clean properly. When they were fighting each other. When they were fighting us. I felt like a daughter on Daughter Days. They were nice.

I feel like I was shifted around a lot as a kid. I liked Carteret and I hated it in some ways too. When I was young it was fun. We just played all over the neighborhood. When it rained we would go to the factory building on Sundays when there were no workers and the whole sloped driveway where the big rigs would back in to fill up whatever was in the warehouse would flood with water. It was like a swimming pool. Me and whomever I was with, the kids around the block, would go play in that filthy water. It was fun as hell. Then we would run out and rip up all the dandelions in the vacant field next to the industrial warehouse.

"Look! We can graffiti with these!" I told my friends.

I'd rip the little yellow flowers off of their stems and smudge them across the big white warehouse. Writing my name and never anything ugly. Just graffiti with dead dandelion heads. I never wanted to really hurt the building or anything, I just wanted to pretend I was graffitiing things. Like a bad girl, I was little. I thought it was a lot of fun. Swimming in the probably toxic rainwater and drawing on the concrete with dandelions.

My grandparents on my dad's side lived right across the street so we would run over to eat pierogis and play in their pool when it was warm out. Way better than the rainwater pool. My grandmother, Babci, was the sweetest old thing. She always had perogies and secret chocolate snacks we would have to ask for, even though we knew where she hid them. My mother says when my Babci first met me she ran up to my mom, a stranger, ripped me right out of her arms, and walked off. My mom says she was taken aback, but my Babci just loved me so much and had been waiting for me to get there. I'm beginning to notice my mom says I've had quite an effect on people. Getting their marriage back together. Bringing my Babci so much anticipation and joy. I don't know if she tells me these things because she knows it will make me feel special or because she wants to believe I'm special. Or maybe she actually does believe I'm special. I wouldn't know. I don't feel as if I've had a mother.

Babci's house was a peculiar place. Very old and Eastern European. All the Mother Marys hanging around with the Pope and such. That silly tacky dining room no one ever ate in. Dido would be there sometimes if he wasn't working in the factory or in the basement watching hockey and, of course, drinking. I really loved him as a child. He always smelled weird, I didn't know what it was. Now I know it was wine or vodka or whatever else he had. He would always slip us twenty-dollar bills.

"Don't tell your dad." He and Babci would insist.

I don't know why they cared. It was just twenty dollars. Probably because he was a pedophile. These aren't the things you know when you graffiti with dandelions. Babci would always feed me. Even when I wasn't hungry she would say I'm too skinny and feed me some grilled cheese sandwiches with strawberry jelly on them or meat stuffed in cabbage, those were my favorite. I love that stuff even to this day.

I hate them both now. Her for protecting a monster and him for being one. I tried to murder him, but the alcoholism got to him first. Sometimes I just want to go back to toxic rainwater and dandelions.

My First Episode In The Green House

I had my first episode in my room upstairs in the greenhouse. I was twelve years old. I remember it like it was yesterday. Every feeling, the smell, and the green carpet crunched beneath my feet.

I had gotten into some sort of argument with my parents. That's the only thing I can't recall - what the argument was about. Probably something childish. Probably something an 8-year-old would argue about, who knows? All I know is I was sent to my room upstairs, you know, that room with the fucking spiders.

I stormed up there in a fury. I was so angry at first. It was just anger at first, normal 8-year-olds anger. Something that calls for, maybe, a tantrum. But when I got upstairs something clicked in my brain. Something I had never felt in my short life. It was a distinct shift. It was the very first time my little body felt rage. The normal anger erupted into some evil type of rage. I don't think my little body could handle it. It couldn't process it. I immediately felt like I was out of my body. I felt like I was a completely different human being.

A monster took over. A demon came out. I ripped everything off of the walls. I tore the sheets off the bed. I tried ripping the pillows apart. I smushed my face into a pillow and screamed until my lungs burnt with fire. Like I said, a demon. I threw everything I could grab, frantic. Out of control. Something else had control. I kicked, screamed, cried, and smashed my head into the wall.

Not a normal tantrum. My blood boiled hot. It felt like my blood was boiling. Now I know where that term comes from. I remember after destroying everything I could it wasn't enough. I felt confused. I felt like the rage had to go somewhere and no place to put it.

11

Feeling possessed, I scanned the room. Like a shark seeking blood. I had a beautiful glass hedgehog with very sharp icicle-looking things on top of its cute head. It was all glass, shiny, a beautiful little hedgehog decoration in a little girl's bedroom. Still feeling like a violent marionette, not in control, out of my body.

Someone else pulling the strings - I leaped for my beautiful little hedgehog. I flipped it upside down, hedgehog spiky head down, and pushed it deep into my little girl's flesh. Dragged it franticly down my arm.

"Yes. THAT feels GOOD Rachael." My brain told me so. I scraped and carved at my arm until the blood drew. Once I saw the blood and my arm stung with warmth and pain the rage vanished. Whatever was making me destroy everything, whatever was pulling the strings, was very satisfied with the pain and the blood. So much so that it crept away swiftly, satiated.

Gave me back control and shot me straight back into my body like an insane DMT trip. I felt complete calmness. What I can only describe as peace. I sat on the bed feeling very confused but still at peace. It's dizzying. I don't think a little brain, any brain for that matter, can handle the emotion of violent murderous rage only to quickly drop into tranquility.

Only eight or so years old. Did everyone do this? I had never seen anything about self-harm. I didn't even know it existed. But when whatever that was, whoever that was, took over I knew exactly what to do to make the chaos cease. I guess I would come to know that feeling over and over and over and over and over again as I got older. Always getting stronger and getting more severe. Until I would one day have a complete psychotic break. I remember when I first saw a doctor because life was becoming so unmanageable. The suicide attempts getting too close together to explain to the family. He sat me down and asked, "Why are you here?"

And I explained the whole twelve years beforehand. For an hour and a half.

SIGNED, NOT LOVED

"Have you ever tried to commit suicide? Which time? How many times?" Doctor asked.

"I lost count. Six that were severe. First at fourteen. Last… a year ago," I replied.

We sat for a long time and at the end of the intake exam he just stared at me and asked, "And you've never seen a therapist? Or a psychiatrist?"

"Nope," I replied.

"Rachael I'm surprised you're alive right now," The doctor said.

 "Well, I'm here now," I told him.

I couldn't explain the rollercoaster, the depression, the mania, and the episodes for most of my life. I could never make anyone around me realize what was happening to me. I didn't even know what was happening to me. I just couldn't explain any of it. Only now can I explain some of it. Only now can I, sometimes, see it coming. Decades of out of body experiences where I'm just a pretty little thing one second and the next I'm smashing my head through a mirror at my reflection.

Eight years old. Before the alcohol. Before the drugs. Before the bullies. Before the boys. Before the girls. I truly believe that was the last day I was completely pure and innocent. That was the day, the first episode, where I met the thief that would rob much of my childhood.

She made quite the entrance.

That awfully sneaky fucking bitch, suffering.

I Never Liked Ghosts or Nazis or Bullies

I never liked school. Wait, that's a lie. I LOVED school. At first. I loved learning and reading. I loved listening to what the teacher was saying. I still remember my kindergarten teacher. Mrs. Dodakowski. I don't think that's how you spell her name, but anyhow. She had a similar name to me which I thought was cool when I was younger. Carteret Public School. Very close to Staten Island. Lots of Eastern European kids. I friended her on Facebook when I was in my twenties. I loved that she remembered me. She and my high school English teacher, Mrs. Matlack, always believed in me.

Mrs. Matlack said I was a good writer. I must have been fourteen, or fifteen years old. I promised her one day I was going to write a book of my own. That I would go back to that nightmare of a town and hand her a copy. I hope she's still around when I finish this.

The teachers always believed in me at first. When I still loved school, before the bullying, before I started acting out before I fell into the ugly cracks of public school systems. Pushed and prodded by mean kids who wouldn't know what decency was if it bit them right in the fucking face.

Before I started unscrewing our little pencil sharpeners, the pretty neon-colored ones were just small enough to twist with one hand and sharpen a pencil with the other hand. Unscrewing the one little screw that held it together so I could get the razor blades out and go to the bathroom and cut my legs up while the English teacher talked about the research paper that was due. There was never a rhyme or reason for the bullying. I was pointed at and laughed at in the hall by a group of girls and boys.

"She's so prude." They cackled to each other.

"Do you know she doesn't even have a boyfriend? She's never even kissed a boy! What a loser!" They remarked.

I ignored them but they were so very persistent. It was weird because I would get bullied for being a prude. Then when I was very slutty I got bullied for being slutty, for my hair no matter the color, my clothes no matter the style. I was bullied for being too quiet, being too loud, being straight edge, for drinking, for not knowing how to smoke weed, even for being high all the time. It's so weird. Kids will literally try and ruin someone's day, someone's life, over anything. I hate kids. I hate teenagers. I hate bullies. I've never had a maternal instinct because all kids are fucking assholes. From the age of ten to twenty-something, selfish, useless, assholes push shy quiet girls into lockers.

When my parents moved me to a small rural town in northern New Jersey that was the worst. That's where the evilest kids walked the halls. That's where I ate my lunch in the bathroom stall just to avoid everyone. I would cut myself up, just on the legs so no one would see when I came out of the stall. But I could feel the blood dripping down my leg all day. It was annoying but it made their words hurt less.

"She's hot. I would fuck her. But she's weird, so I won't." That's what they said about me. Someone literally told me that once. At fifteen.

There were only a couple of kids in my years that were ever truly nice to me. Azalea, like the flower, lived next to my grandparent's house. Across the street from me in Carteret. My first real friend. We would play with Bratz Dolls up in her room. I would smush mine together and make them make out and have what I thought was sex. Just smashing them together over and over again. Thinking maybe I would do that one day so the boys and girls at school would stop bullying me.

My other friend was Katie. Her parents were nice and she had long blonde hair and blue eyes. She never made fun of me and we got along really well. I went back to Carteret to visit her years later. We sat in her backyard, and many years later, both grew into beautiful women. I liked seeing her. I liked that the town that just kept getting worse and worse didn't chew her up and spit her out. I went back to visit Azalea one time too when I was at my grandparent's house. I knocked on the door. But she wasn't home. I think she had a child and that's about all I know.

Then there was Nikita. She was a few blocks from me and when I was old enough my parents would let me ride my bike to her house as long as I was back before the street lights came on. She had two brothers. I remember having a crush on one of them. That was the first time, I think, that I thought of a boy like that. Not sexually but just that I liked his face and when he was around I would act extra cool because he was older. One time Nikita and I had a sleepover and watched Pet Cemetery in the dark in her living room. I hate that fucking movie. It was so scary. There we were, small, young, and scared, on the edge of the couch. I was clutching the blanket so hard covering both of my eyes with it so I could barely see the screen. There was a little window right above where I was sitting, shaking. Then a loud BANG came from the window. I screamed and nearly pissed myself. It was her big brother. Banging on the window because he knew we were having a sleepover and watching something scary. I hated him for doing that. I can never watch that movie again. To this day. I hate even thinking about Pet Cemetery. But I still had a crush on her brother.

I went back to my grandparent's house to see my Babci because I liked seeing her and I knew she was getting sick. She's fought breast cancer so many times I've lost count. She's an iron woman. Death can't take her. A tough Polish potato. I'll be genuinely surprised when she dies even though she is very old. When she was in Poland she got crushed by a machine in the factory. Crushed her hips and they said she'd never have children. But she did. Kind of like when my mom had problems with her ovaries and they said she'd never had kids, but she did. I feel like we were all just never supposed to exist. But somehow we did. All down the line of Kaliczynski's. Not really supposed to be here but kind of supposed to be here.

SIGNED, NOT LOVED

My great-grandmother had it hard too, Babci Zima. She and I lived long enough to meet each other and sit and talk. Her house smelled old but comfortable. She would hug and kiss me and say I was too skinny and that I had to eat more food. Thick Polish accent. She just loved me so much I could feel it. Even though a Nazi raped her a long time ago to make my grandmother, who made my father, who made me. Kind of damned. Babci Zima's husband's side of the family didn't like us much, I don't think. Not for any real reason. But I guess back then rape was the woman's fault and we were just products of that. The worst of us in Poland was when the Nazis came through and raped her and made my grandma a product of evil.

My Babci didn't deserve anything other than worship for being so strong and so kind in the midst of such terrible things. And her mother, a saint, Babci Zima. Giving the best life she could to a baby that no one wanted. Those two women are fucking saints. I don't believe in saints but they are saints. They deserve every level of heaven and every comfort in the afterlife. Because they smiled and cleaned and made perogies and taught me Christmas carols and never mentioned the bad men in our lives. They made everything better even when it really wasn't.

That's a saint. I'll twist God's arm myself if He doesn't have the best spot for Babci and Babci Zima in Heaven. I'll raise hell and howl at Jesus, the Son of God.

"Have you seen what they've been through?! Give them everything they want. Look what they fucking did. Look what was fucking done to them while they smiled and made cookies and put flowers in our hair, Jesus. You make the rest of their eternity better than the rest of us. Give them the best seat. Give them all my heavenly stuff and places and room. Just let them have peace, Jesus, because you fucking know what they went through." And I would say it. I would scream and yell and shout at God Himself to give those fucking women whatever they want. But God isn't real and I don't like to yell anymore.

Anyway. I guess I liked visiting Dido too, but I always had a sick ugly feeling when he was around. I think my consciousness knew he was a bad man without me really knowing. Without really remembering. Before I knew he would throw my Babci down the stairs when he was drunk. Before I knew a lot of the times she was in the hospital if it wasn't the breast cancer, it was because of that piece of shit. Before he tried to fuck me when I was a kid.

So I would visit her and hope he wasn't there. Walked to Nikita's house, still knowing the streets like the back of my hand. That's what I love the most about growing up before smartphones. I knew where I was going all the time. I never had anything to look at. Don't get me wrong, I won't walk a block without my iPhone. I'll feel anxiety overcoming me as soon as I walk down the apartment stairs. If I make it to the pharmacy without it I can feel that panic in the back of my mind. Such as "What if I need to call someone? What if I don't remember where I live? What if someone attacks me or I get hurt? Irrational things. I wouldn't go back to those days of riding around on my bike, knowing."

Exactly where I was going. That's what nostalgia is for.

Anyway, I visited Nikita. Knocked on her door. Her mom answered. "Hey. I'm Rachael. I used to be good friends with Nikita. Does she still live here? This might be weird. I was in town and just wanted to say hi."

"Oh, Rachael!"

She hugged me. "I remember you!" She asked how I was doing and what I was up to. I can't remember what job I had back then but I told her I was living in New York City and such and such. I guess I said enough to impress her. I guess it was nice I hadn't gotten knocked up or strung out on drugs (yet) or failed really early in life or something like that. I just failed consistently.

"Wow. You look beautiful. I'll tell her you came by," Nikita mother said. In the back of my head, I'm wondering if her brother is still around, if he's still a dick that would scare two little girls, and if he's still attractive because if he saw me now, maybe I would get laid. Not romantically. Just an old memory that I stirred up and made sexual because I was in my twenties, hot, and didn't care. Instead, we had some short small talk and I left.

I walked back towards my grandparent's house and stopped across the street at the house I grew up in. Before we moved to a small town in northern New Jersey that was supposed to be nicer and supposed to be safer. Nowhere is fucking safe. My mom moved us because the town was getting worse and our schools had metal detectors. I just stood there. Looking at some house that another family probably lived in now.

I got a sick but alluring feeling looking at that stupid greenhouse. Kind of smushed too close to the others on the block. It was like looking at that certain type of booze you drank way too much of one night. Remembering the good times. But you'll vomit if you take the cap off. You'll vomit if you go inside and smell it.

I'm pretty sure that house is haunted. It was when I was little for sure and I'm sure eviler festered there through the years I lived there. I don't really believe in ghosts. I do believe in negative and positive energies. My older sister used to say she could feel them. She told me stories about what happened in that house. One time she was in the kitchen and out of nowhere felt surrounded by things. Very dark and very angry things. Hundreds of them she said. All squeezed in our tiny kitchen surrounding her, staring at her. They encroached, making her feel like she was being told to leave. She ran out of that house. I don't know if she told anyone else.

I was always very vocal about anything and everything I felt, saw, heard, and smelled. I think that's why she was a good kid. Never caused any trouble. Sometimes I should have just kept my fucking mouth shut.

I was paranoid about living in that house. At a very young age constantly in fear of what I couldn't see in the living room or the kitchen or the basement or anywhere else. Perhaps I should have welcomed them. Because the things

I could not see in the living room or the kitchen or the basement or anywhere else were never as evil, ever as dangerous, as the things that were in the living room or the kitchen or the basement or anywhere else.

I'm sure that attributes to my paranoia now. Some little breadcrumb in the long trail of things leading to why I have to take fucking pills every day to function like a normal person, but not quite. I panicked all the time about the spiders in my rooms and sometimes I would sneak downstairs to my grandma's room and sleep there and my parents would get upset, but that room, that green carpet the voices, the Hedgehog, the spiders. My mom heard stuff too. Running up and down the stairs. To the point, she thought someone broke in all the time because we lived in a bad area. So she would grab the gun and go to the basement and confront it, but nothing was ever there. I hate that town. That house. That green carpet.

Hackettstown, NJ 2011-ish

Strippers Are Better Than Car Salesmen

I never planned to be a stripper. I don't know if any woman ever does Sits down, all options in front of her and decides to climb a golden pole instead of a corporate ladder. I don't find it a demeaning job. I pity those who do. Those who don't know what it's like to make an honest living off of a dishonest man's dime.

I was eighteen when I first tried. I had bartended at a seedy place that served Legs and Eggs but I was new, fresh, and different than the dancers. I was untouchable and I just made the drinks. I think that's what made the customers want me more.

"Can I get a dance with her?" Customers often asked.

The manager would ask me. I wasn't pushed to it because I was hired to tend the bar but I could if I wanted to. But it was double. I always declined until one day, I don't know what changed my mind. Maybe I had something in mind I wanted to buy that I couldn't afford. Either way, it was strange to me and awkward but I was apparently a natural. I liked that. So I continued as a bartender, giving doubly expensive dances here and there. Eventually, I got confident though and wanted to be up on stage. Wanted to know what it was like to be up there, hands smelling of rubbing alcohol and body smelling of coconut vanilla lotion. We used the rubbing alcohol to spray down the pole, so we never slipped and our thighs could grip it while we fell backward, slowly, and gracefully.

Suspended only by our tight legs, our hair falling, just gliding along the stage. The good poles weren't stationarity, they spun. So we would hold form like that. Upside down and spinning like a beautiful ornament, like a morbid mobile above a child's crib meant to soothe their cries but instead, we soothed old men's minds just for a moment.

21

The first time I did it I was hooked. I felt untouchable up there. I would swing, flip, climb to the very top of the pole where I could touch the ceiling, and then let go, drop down to the stage when the chorus hit, a loud BANG of my black latex knee-high stilettos would startle the entire bar. Very slowly stand up. Toss the hair out of my face. Smirk at their amazement and a little bit of fear. Nine Inch Nails blasting through a cheap sound system. Damn, I get butterflies even now thinking about it. I love that feeling.

I told my mom I served drinks at a restaurant that never existed. Eventually, she found out. That's when I lied. Said I moved in with a girlfriend and had my own place. Disappeared, I was an adult. Right?

My mother wasn't stupid. I would go to work wearing sweats, a baggy t-shirt, clutching a big duffle bag with an assortment of colorful sometimes latex and silky outfits. I loved my job. I think. At the time.

I was young and naive. I hadn't the bite and confidence and knowledge of self-worth to do the job the right way. That was before the drugs, the robbing, and the darkness. Stripping never got me into drugs. I mean, they were there. But I wasn't interested. I was honestly just trying to make a living in a world I liked much better than what the other girls were doing. I didn't like being a secretary or waitress. I didn't want to greet people at car dealerships like some prop to make people throw thousands of dollars on something. I never wanted to be a girl working at a car dealership. Those were the jobs I hated my friends took the most for some reason. Looking pretty in a lot. Trying to make men spend money. Staring at a parade of old, new, used, fun things to drive just to make themselves feel better...oh wait. Buying a car is a lot like being at a strip club. Pick your make, model, and year.

I think that was my first taste of a woman's body being a commodity. You always start at the bottom though. Tacky shoes with a firm flaunt but unsure eyes. It takes years to learn how to grab a man by his throat for touching you without permission. It takes seasons to catch their lies, avoid the rapes, and learn how to say "Wow, I would never speak to you the way your wife does." All while wondering what she's up to while her husband sips a cheap-ass Coors Light and caresses your fishnets. You're bored. You're not turned on or turned off. You're working. You may think it's different but your dull day job is just a nine to five even when you're a stripper too. Just because your office talk takes place near a water cooler over some coffee while I'm talking to Lashes about the way she decided to shave her bush that day doesn't make it much different.

It's still 10 AM. We're still tired. We still had to commute. We still have to pay the phone bill tomorrow. Lashes were my favorite. She worked there the longest, and was younger than me, or at least seemed it. But she was a tough fucking cookie. Everyone knew her. She was always kind to me and the new girls. That's how you knew a good stripper colleague, not the ones who got jealous or hazed the scared new ones. The Lashes were sweet. I loved talking to her. My smelly wrinkled cash is stacked as nicely as it could next to me on the bench that I'm straddling in the dressing room. Hair straightener in one hand while I iron the cash with it. "You know what? I'm going to shave it into a W," Lashes said.

I think she was wearing something silky and blue. She liked things with long tails of fabric that followed her around like snakes. "A W? Why? That seemed really difficult," I replied.

"For Wu-Tang." She jiggled her little white butt. God, she was so cute. I would not fuck with her, but she was still cute.

RACHAEL MADORI

The money steams.

Finally straight enough so the bank accountant might not assume things. A stripper's salary clutched between a hot hair irons has a specific smell.

I remember it.

I loved it more than your morning coffee.

I was very young and ignorant at first. I've worked across the country from small-town redneck hideouts to platinum-plus high-baller clubs and to be honest I made the most in the dirtiest of places, I'm not sure why. I never liked the really high-end places, the ones that made me wear a gown and float through the club like some goddess. I'm not sure why but it was irritating. It seemed fake. I know it's all fake but that was fake on top of fake. My favorite spots were the places where I worked lunch. In a small town. Not much going on elsewhere. I would shoot the shit for hours with men.

Hanging out, the sun is beaming but it is pitch black in the club. Every time me and the manager went out for a cigarette the sun would blind the room for a moment cracking through the door. We would close it as quickly as possible so everyone could keep to the illusion that there wasn't one outside.

She was a fierce, fiery older woman in her late forties, I think, with long red hair. I wish I remembered her name. We fell out hard when I left. I can't remember exactly why but she was like a mom to me when I was there. She was tough and made her own way. She was loud and drove a convertible. I think she was the baddest, strongest, not give a fuck what men said woman I had ever met at that age. That's probably why I looked at her like a mom for some time. Really looked up to her like a daughter. I hope she's doing well.

I was always friends with the DJs. They ran the show. Your music. Your vibe. When you got up there, he's like your big brother over there in the booth. I loved that shit. I guess they were like my family you could say. The manager, the DJs, the girls. I never felt like I had much of a family back home. Which sounds sad now. Because I had a mom, dad, and three sisters.

SIGNED, NOT LOVED

Maybe wondering where I had gone. Why I had disappeared. Only show up once in a while so they knew I was alive. Or because I had to do laundry. For then I had a new one though and to this day… I still love them all like family.

The men, would sneak in during work or just before going home. They spent the most money. More than the drunk ballers coming in on Fridays and Saturdays. Being loud and buying bottles. I avoided them while the other girls flocked. No shame that was their way. They made good money with them. I never did. Even when they wanted to talk to me. Their conversations bored me. They acted like they had it all figured out and treated me like I owed them something.

I liked the old guys. Who just wanted to sit and talk. And yeah, sometimes got too handy, and sometimes ended up being very bad men who take advantage of a young stripper in the lap dance room because she didn't know. But most of them were good men. Just lonely. Very lonely.

We talked about our plans. Their lives. Most of the men would buy lap dances just to have a place to talk for hours. A pretty thing on his lap that was listening. I don't know what it was like with the other girls. Because I actually felt for them. At first. I wanted to be their therapist and they would come back asking for advice and I would give it. With a cocktail, a warm cheek on their leg, and a couple of twenty dollar bills. I've heard every story about every wife and every child and every annoying thing that made you come here. Sometimes they would just come to have a beer and see new moves I was practicing. They wouldn't even touch me. They were my friends. I even told them my real name. They paid for my stuff but I was more involved in their lives than I was in anyone else I have ever met. They would trust me to watch their car, or their dog or pick their lottery ticket.

I still know the flow of the club. How it works. I miss it sometimes. It's a really comfortable feeling there. No matter the city or the girls or the state, I know the hierarchy, and how everything works together. I kept quiet or stood up for other dancers when I could. Fight when I had to but I didn't like it. Maybe I liked it a little.

It was like a sisterhood. And those were some of the kindest, most real women you'll ever know. I loved their kids, I hated their shit boyfriends and I would kill anyone who followed them in the parking lot. They fucking knew what life was. I would look out for new ones. When I dipped in and out of different clubs at different ages and different states. Fuck, even writing this I miss it. One of the best jobs of my life. Those women are tough as nails. That shit is like a secret society.

Everywhere you go.

I don't even want to spill all of our secrets and ways. Because we deserve our ways.

I would do it again.

No matter how successful I get.

If Nine Inch Nails plays on the sound system, I'll think of Lashes, and hope she made it too.

Fired

I got fired from my first dream job. I was in deep active addiction.

Shooting up in grocery store parking lots.

But I got a restaurant management job at a nice place. Where I was for the first and only time fired.

Too many trips to the bathroom.

Too many times I got stuck in Paterson and couldn't make it to work. I cried when she sat across from me and let me go.

I screamed, copped drugs, shot up in a grocery store sparkling lot, and auditioned at a strip club.

Things went pretty downhill from there.

Sweet Sixteen

My mother made a beautiful cake for my sweet sixteen. My father decorated the house and made so much food. I dressed up my best.

And I sat.

And sat.

For hours.

I caught the glimpse of realization in my parent's exchange. They knew.

No one was coming. So I left.

And got drunk.

Because that's how I dealt with things ever since I was 14.

Silver Mouth

I sat with the .357 in my mouth for an hour. Pushing myself for the courage to pull the trigger. The taste of metal was chilly.

I crawled home crying. Handed it to my mother. "You're fucking stupid."

We never, ever spoke about it again.

Hollywood, CA 2014-ish

Showers

I love showers.

I love bathrooms.

I've always loved them.

I said to Chef once

"Hey, I want to go out classy! Slit wrists in a porcelain white tub.

Gorgeous. So Hollywood!"

I don't think he liked that comment.

But I was overwhelmed today and I didn't know where to go. When that happens I always go in the shower.

Like my old dog when he's having a spell, he sneaks into the standing shower and curls up.

Hiding where it's cool and quiet. I did that today.

I loved it.

SIGNED, NOT LOVED

The second the warm water hits my body and my dark hair gets like the Grudge girl. Sometimes I stand with my head against the tiles and let the water slide down my ass. Sometimes I just sit on the gross linoleum floor and look at the tiles. There's something about the escape of a shower or a bath I'm in love with. I soaked in my mother-in-law's deep spa tub, she made me a bubble bath, soaking and swishing, watching the trees in north New Jersey escape.

I drank an entire bottle of 99 Bananas Vodka when I was 17 in Seaside Heights, at the Jersey Shore in a tub too. They were my little escapes. The one in Hollywood I can't remember, I'm trying to but I can't. Too many drugs then, I think.

Sylmar's shower was amazing, with dark tiles, and a sliding glass door. I could just stay in there all night and day. I like coming out and wiping the fog off the mirror, always thinking someone new might be looking back. Obviously, there never is but it's a fun game. Ah. Just stare at yourself in the bathroom mirror. I fucking love bathrooms. Silent. White. Porcelain. Steamy. Stories only you know in there.

Why do you think people sing in the shower? It's a thing! It's a special place. I'd like to die there. Anywhere with the warm water, bubbles. If it's soon in my own hand it'll be red and beautiful.

If it's when I'm old and dying maybe it'll be a sad nap and I'll drown. I'm going to keep enjoying my showers and bathrooms and porcelain. I'll keep wondering why I love the idea of blood all over it too.

Who knows? I'll just keep watching the tiles and loving the slippery heat of the water. Showers are sexy. Bathroom deaths are sexy.

It's Coming (Again)

I can feel the depression trying to take hold.

The creepiest part of mental illness is when you're a year into recovery but can tell an episode is coming.

The smell before a tornado, the last gasp of air before going under the water.

It's still, silent, And absolutely terrifying.

Roofies

I've been roofied a few times. But the best, was when I was drugged at a club in Los Angeles. And woke up in my apartment in Brooklyn.

The last thing I remember is my heel sliding into the Uber.

Black.

Nothing.

Until I woke to the sounds of sirens.

"This doesn't sound like my Hollywood apartment." I look up.

I guess I'm staying in New York.

RACHAEL MADORI

Pornstars

We were young, wild, and free.

Buy a convertible for a weekend in Vegas crazy. But we all had our ways and we made our way.

Dropped a stack at my nail tech that day.

Fast money is a fun world with no rules to obey. Parties in the Hollywood Hills every day.

The mansions and champagne were clean and fine.

I remember the taste of every other cocaine line. Bottles to spare, bare assed down the stairwell. Get drunk in green rooms and yell out rappers' names. Fuck them later and tell all your friends.

Lived in the lights and nights but I never saw darkness. And I deserved that ignorant bliss on my conscious. I wouldn't choose to have lived my twenties any other way.

I was a different kind of beautiful back then, wild and dumb of tomorrow. I wouldn't trade the world to rid myself of its beautiful sorrow.

34

New Therapist

When you meet a new therapist for the millionth time it's usually awkward and boring.

This time it was both. But with a bit of intrigue. Because he's young.

Not my type, so I didn't think.

But I'm coming to like men I didn't use to like. I used to not like men much at all.

But Jasmine, my friend, likes her employee because it's wrong and she's in charge.

So now I sympathize with her because I want to fuck my shrink. Because technically he's in charge.

And now in his field of study.

If I got him to do it I would be in charge. It would be wrong.

It would feel good.

He has a literary background.

He likes Bukowski and is familiar with him. This turns me on more.

He's not my usual type. Glasses. Sweater. White. No tattoos.

Older than me but not by much.

I know he's there to help me. I want him to help me.

I also want to know if he would break the rules with me.

 I read him my poetry, to try and show him how I feel.

He liked it.

RACHAEL MADORI

He likes my poetry which is flattering.

I want to know if he would break rules for me.

I think it's a control thing.

I think it would be nice to dominate him.

Get him out of his shell and do something wrong.

He seems to stand up though. Like he wouldn't do it.

It's like a game.

I don't think he knows he's in.

I'm going to dress much sexier next time I see him. And talk more about poetry and Bukowski.

I want to know if he's attracted to me too.

I tell my husband when I get home.

He laughs.

But I'm not evil.

I don't want to ruin this man's life. I just want to see if he would do it. If he would cross that line.

I don't think he would. He's very professional.

But what is it in me that makes me want to find out?

Heels

One time The LAPD found me running

All the way down I-405 with nothing but a pair of heels on

Kind of how they would find me Wandering around Brooklyn

In my pink bathrobe High on PCP

They would bring me home like a lost puppy.

Brooklyn, NY 2017-ish

Morbib Accordion

I get in from a double work night, 10 AM to 10 PM. I have some kind of Bronchitis, and I am feeling like shit. I'm broke and have to take the bus to the subway because I'm in credit card debt. I actually just paid off all my credit card debt, but then my score shot up to 780 and they sent me a new one. One with 8,000 on it. So I'm sore with a new tattoo sleeve. But I'm still broke. Just hood rich. But I'm tired, and at least if I get in an Uber, I won't go to a bar.

I get high because maybe it'll make me feel better. PCP isn't really what my doctor would recommend. 40 thnx, the blue text bubble pops up and sends to my husband. So he knows how much I want to be weighed out. So it's waiting for me when I get home. Still coughing up one or both of my lungs. It usually chills me out. Plus, I can't pick up my prescription medication until Monday. This also doesn't matter because I'll get high whether I had my medication tonight or not.

He wants to show me a cool video. A complete history of the Soviet Union arranged to the melody of Tetris. He likes weird things like that. I slouch down on the blue couch next to him to watch.

Eastern European music brings about a massive accordion piece in the background. Traditional.

That sound.

I haven't heard it in ages, since I was a child.

I feel warmth in my chest and acid in my gut. Why am I going to cry over this stupid YouTube video?

Everything starts feeling compressed. I'm breathing heavier.

SIGNED, NOT LOVED

Why can't I catch my breath?

Flashes of milky memories start to leak into my mind. That sound.

I haven't heard it in ages.

Since I was a child. Singing and dancing in the dusty basement of my grandfather. The sound rapes my mind. Ripping memories I had long forgotten. Some are so beautiful and innocent. Like when my grandpa, I called him Dido, would show my little fingers how to pull and push and play the accordion. Or when I would watch him drunkenly sing and serenade us. His cheeks were red and slippery like the accordion. Red and slippery like the bar in the basement I would pop up on. Too little to sit up there, they said.

"What's this?" A wall of obscure booze faces me. I know it's what the grown-ups drink, but he'll always let me have a taste if I ask. There's a mug with a woman's ass hanging in the center, like a Hawaiian woman doing the Hulu dance. When you fill it and drink from it, the ass wiggles. I flicked it. I thought it was funny. I still think it's funny only because he's dead.

I just called my dad before this whole mess in my head. Told him how happy I was when I met some new friends. We made food for the Fourth of July. Really made food with our hands. I felt high with my hands in the cabbage or when I was slapping the cookie dough onto the baking sheet. I got excited to call my Dad to tell him I got this nostalgic feeling being in the kitchen, shooting the shit with other women, cooking, and making something nice like the ladies did when I was a child. I have great memories of being a child.

My dad knows what the accordion means. He knows why I had a panic attack when the sound sucked up memories carpeted deep inside my brain.

"Tell your husband why you're crying. Be open. He should know," My dad advised.

"It's a late night, Dad. He's tired. I'm tired," I replied, knowing I was just dragging more dust under the carpet.

39

RACHAEL MADORI

I keep apologizing for calling him again and again so late. He always tells me to stop it; that I can call any time. He's always there for me. Even when he's not, I'll keep apologizing for calling him because this hurts him too.

I call my dad to tell him the sound of an accordion sent me into a panic attack because it railed me with memories of happy times dancing and singing with Dido, his father, and my grandfather, but it's morbid.

Because memories of his father only get a split second of happiness. Then reality kicks in. Then we all remember. Then we both have to remember that Dido would show my little fingers how to pull and push and play the accordion when I was a child to the tunes of our Eastern European ancestors.

But that Dido would pull me and push his tongue down my throat. That's why it's morbid.

Because sometimes, the accordion was a happy sound when I was young and didn't know what alcohol was. Who the alcoholics were. What the alcoholics did.

The accordion was fun when I was so tiny I couldn't hold and squeeze the damned thing to make the music right. But the man who played it, that wasn't fun. When he thought he could hold and play and squeeze me.

All of this, on a random night on PCP after watching a stupid YouTube video, I call my Dad and cry and laugh and say, "This book is going to be fucking awesome. But I think I just scared my husband." My dad says to talk about it, be open and get it out, and write.

I did. We walked the dogs down a Brooklyn street while I reminded him that evil grandfathers exist. He already knows most of my life. He just didn't know the accordion would send me over the edge. It doesn't matter anymore, though. Because I just did another line of PCP, and we're watching what rich Saudi women are doing on Snapchat.

My husband says

SIGNED, NOT LOVED

"I'm sitting on top of clouds right now."

I like when he's happy. Sober or high, I just like when he's happy.

Because at least someone doesn't have a panic attack when they hear an accordion.

Brunch

"Sasha? Gaara? Rachael? Hello? Does anyone care that I'm home?" My husband voice echoed.

"I'm here, in the guest room, writing! I love you. You know that I'm just distracted," I replied.

"Well, I feel bad because I cut my workout short because I wanted to come home and see you, but now I know I shouldn't have cut my workout short because I feel bad," He responded with guilt in his voice.

"You had a good workout. You shouldn't feel bad," I replied, trying to console him.

"But I do always feel bad when I cut my workout short, and I keep thinking about it," he responded in such a cute voice.

"Well, that's because you have Body Dysmorphia and OCD and should be seeing a therapist," I replied.

I don't remember what he said after that, but everything I said was true.

We're having this conversation while I swipe back and forth between writing and Instagram and Snapchat and emailing back John's that might help me pay off my credit card debt. He'll ask about my John Work sometimes, but only when he needs the details to ensure I'm safe.

Otherwise, it is my business that I run for myself. I mean for ourselves. Because the extra money is nice, and there are a lot of rich, bored men in New York City. Meanwhile, our conversation continued with him asking "How's your writing going?"

"Good."

"Am I bothering you with my words?"

"Yes."

SIGNED, NOT LOVED

"I miss you."

God, I love this man more than life itself.

I close the guest room door. I'm lying in bed typing, and he's now cursing at the video games, which annoys the hell out of me, but he works such long hours in such a soul-beating, a mentally sickening, and fulfilling job so I don't bother him for his irritating video game noises on his days off. Also, I'm wondering why I'm writing in bed in the guest room when I should be in the office. But I guess that's where I just study my wine.

Wow.

What a cunt.

26 years old, and I get to work on my book in my guest room in bed with my dementia-ridden Shih Tzu and squirrelly Chiweenie but study my wine career in my office. My friends would call me a fucking bitch and laugh and take Instagram stories while we drank pisco sours at brunch, talking about how I lucked out on nabbing this apartment before the gentrification in this area so I could afford such a place.

It would be funny, and they would be slightly envious but, in all, truly happy for me because they're strong independent women too, and we love each other with all of our individual successes and individual flaws. It would be an amazing brunch on a rooftop somewhere in Williamsburg in July.

But I don't have any friends.

So I'm going to crawl out on my fire escape and see if this Camel cigarette will help my pneumonia.

RACHAEL MADORI

Beethaoven Wobble Legs

He fucked me so good I fell off the bed

Onto the dirty wooden floor Hair a mess

Dangling over my face I shouted

"Turn down the Beethoven, it's too fucking loud!"

He says "What we just did was loud, who cares about the Beethoven!"

"Just turn it down for our neighbors and help me up you motherfucker."

So he turned down Beethoven.

Me on the floor, collapsed after many orgasms. The dogs look at me crazy,

They act weird when we have sex. It was a good night.

Tar

Insufflated 40mg of DPT, also known as The Light. It is a psychedelic drug belonging to the tryptamine family. DPT is used as a religious sacrament by the Temple of the True Inner Light, a New York City offshoot of the Native American Church. The Temple believes DPT and other entheogens are physical manifestations of God.

I am fluid.

I leak darkness over the edges and spill slowly along the couch. I am heavy and black.

Sludge, slug, over your arms. Seeping to the floor.

I lick the bottom.

Black.

I melt.

My toes turn to black, slowly they slither.

The feeling beneath my toes is thick. I cannot move.

I am trapped in this muck of dirty. Save me.

It creeps from the couches fabric. It straps me up.

I am in its claws.

What is it?

Dog Treats

Peanut butter dog treats. Perogies on the floor.

PCP dust everywhere. Vaseline lips.

Bose speaker is too loud at 4 AM because that's MY time.

I keep telling everyone at work to just

Buy me a

Coffin, and I'll stay in

It all day,

Comfy.

Wheel me out at 4 PM for the world. Tight hair, blazer, lips, face, pants suit.

I'm like a walking corpse, and they don't even know it. Primped and propped.

Looks great on the outside to see. Embalmed on the inside just for me.

Sometimes Sucking Off in a Boudoir, Sometimes Sniffing a Pinot Noir

I just got out of wine class, where I get to sit, learn and research the Devil's plaything. It's a real mindfuck that I'm addicted to my career. Not in a workaholic sense but in an alcoholic sense. Like the high majority of the people in my industry who don't want to admit it. I am very professional, though, and also very careful. Every time I swirl, sip, and taste, I have to be extremely adamant about using the spit bucket. Every time I can feel the wine slowly trying to slide down my throat.

"Come on. Just a little." My brain teases me. I'm holding back years of alcohol abuse, all while developing my palate for the dauntingly difficult task of deducing a gorgeous wine with my peers. None of them know that every class is just a little bit more difficult for me than for them. And that's okay. I chose to stay in this profession. I chose to tango with the Devil because I'm a decent Sommelier but an even better-functioning alcoholic.

I finish cleaning the phlegmy gurgle and disgusting spit of my peers from the lecture room tables because I'm a TA, a teacher's assistant. It gave me a large discount on my tuition to come early, set up and stay late to clean. My profession may have an elitist lure, but that doesn't make me any less broke.

Today we learned of Burgundy and all its delicious splendor. I think I'm a special kind of sommelier because I've learned to taste and rip apart a wine down to its varying depths of complex flavor and a never-ending spoon of knowledge, all while rarely getting a chance to let it make me warm, drunk, and comfortable. I just have to let it flow across my tongue, luscious and slutty. And then spit it out like a bad fuck. Like when I kicked out that one girl I fell in love with while fucking her with my husband. Because I had to make, the feelings go away. That's what wine is like to me. A dangerous lover I keep coming back to even though one day she could break my heart and I would go to jail for my unrelenting obsession with her.

Anyway. I'm trying to rush home. I just want to get home. I rush up Seventh Ave to the nearest subway. Black heels, skin gripping shin high black dress, big black bag, and hair pulled back tight. My legs are too long to rush with wide strides, so I hike my dress up a good bit and hold it at my side. Do the boys behind me like what they see? Who cares?

Not me.

I'm lying to myself.

I outpace the rest of the dumb-faced tourists around me. I must look exactly how I'm supposed to.

Fucking ridiculous.

But… like I belong.

I strut right by the Pennsylvania Hotel on 33rd and 7th. Huh, forgot that was there. I used to stay there a lot when I was escorting. Waiting in that filthy room with the water-stained ceiling. That was before I was high-end.

Before, I knew which were the best sex-working hotels in the city. Which ones didn't require a key card to get up to my room? Which ones wouldn't notice? I had men coming and going all day. But finally, one day, the hotels weren't as necessary because their penthouses were much more discreet. Fuck Hotel Pennsylvania. I think about how I must be much classier now. Trading tasting notes and sniffing a divine Pinot Noir instead of comparing the last taste of cum to the next sniff of an asshole. Do you want to talk about coming from the bottom? They used to cum on my bottom. Now I look at the bottom of my wine glass,

"Sir, do you find this to be a medium yellow or more of a pale gold?" Simply ridiculous.

My life is a running joke, but I love every moment of it.

Thank God I'm almost to the subway. Sweat is dripping down the middle of my tits, and it's increasingly irritating. A cute lady rushes in front of me. I

48

couldn't hear her because I had my noise-canceling headphones on, blasting some sad song I've had on repeat for the past three days while I locked myself in the office and wrote.

Fuck. I shouldn't have stopped. They always have you for a solid five minutes when you stop if you're not enough of an asshole to tell them to stop bothering you and continue on. I pull my headphones off. Praying she just wants a cigarette or money so I can throw either at her and be on my way. "Hi, we're taking a quick survey."

"Quick. Yeah. Okay," I replied.

"Have you ever imagined the image of God as a woman? The Mother? Instead of a man?"

You have to be fucking kidding me.

"Well yeah. Of course. I think women are inherently nurturing, and it would be much nicer to have the idea of a female God. And who's to say what is and what isn't."

I should have just said I don't believe in God and just made my train.

Her much older colleague steps in. She looks like a sweet grandmother who would sit you down when you're sad and comfort you with some common esoteric ideal that only grandmothers understand.

She goes on and on about how God created the female figure for a reason and, that there are mothers in the animal kingdom, that God could have made just Adam. And Adam could have fathered everything, but He made Eve, so there must be a Mother God. I like what she's saying, and if we were sitting down at a bar chatting, I would get drunk and sit with her for hours talking about religion and philosophy, and the patriarchy.

But we're not. She's not. And the sweat between my tits is staining my dress. "Okay, well, I really have to go."

49

"Well, could we call or email you? You know we have a lot of volunteer opportunities." Her attractive friend next to her is short; she gleams up at me, so excited for their cause.

Fuck.

At least I have my business cards on me, so I have a quick out of this. "Oh my goodness. Yes absolutely. Here is my card. I love volunteering." At least that's not a lie, Rachael. At least you're not a total selfish bitch.

"I do work in suicide prevention. So any chance I get to volunteer for a good cause is always an interest to me."

I sound like a saint, but really, I just wanted them to know I'm not a total degenerate trying to get away from them as quickly as possible.

"So you work for the suicide hotlines?"

UGH. RELEASE ME, ADORABLE WOMAN, WHO I WOULD DEFINITELY BRING BACK TO MY APARTMENT AND GO DOWN ON IF WE WERE UNDER DIFFERENT CIRCUMSTANCES.

"No, I did charity events and public speaking as a suicide survivor raising funds and awareness about suicide and mental illness."

They're intrigued. Great. At least they might have some hope in this filthy city when I walk away.

I give them my card.

"You know we have a blood drive soon." The grandmother says to me.

"Ah. Her tattoos." Her friend points to my arm.

The only genuine excitement I've had during this entire interaction is that she noticed my new tattoos.

"Yeah, sorry, I can't donate blood because they're new. Okay, well, call or email me. I really have to get going!" I wave sweetly and runoff.

50

SIGNED, NOT LOVED

Please don't fucking call me.

I get down to the humid subway track, and, fuck, the train is there, and the doors are just closing.

Of course. Like I said.

My life is a running fucking joke.

RACHAEL MADORI

A Very Normal Day

It seems silly that I pay for very expensive facial treatments. Go to a very fancy place by Grand Central Station.

Walk among very important people doing very important things. Ignoring very dirty people with very big problems.

 The waiting room is very gorgeous, and they make me very delicious ginger tea while I wait.

I talk about my travels with my specialist while I lay in a very comfortable robe.

He's a very genuine man, just trying to keep my face very pretty. I always leave feeling very special and very relaxed.

I take the train home, and slowly the people start looking less impressive.

The streets become very dirty, and I curse very loudly when I realize it will skip my stop.

I hurry down the subway stairs to the bus because I can't afford an Uber home.

My very long, beautiful dress makes it very difficult to catch public transportation while running.

 I make it home just in time before I have to do that again, so I can work very late all night long.

I love my neighborhood because it isn't very nice, but it is very real, and that's my favorite.

I strip down to my panties as soon as I get in because it's very hot in New York in July.

SIGNED, NOT LOVED

And sweat drips down my newly glowing face that I paid very too much money for while I clean up a very large amount of piss that my dog has left on the floor for me.

Don't Lie About PCP

God, can pneumonia kill you? My lungs feel like they're filled with the Hudson. Disgusting gurgling water every time I take a breath. I'm in an Uber heading to a 24-Hour Clinic in Brooklyn to finally get some meds. It's 11 PM, and my Uber driver probably thinks I am disgusting. I'm covering my face with my shirt in the backseat.

His name is Tarique. I don't think I'm spelling his name correctly. I know his name now because I got out and tried to get into the hospital, and this side of it was closed. So Tarique stayed in the hospital lane and rolled down the window.

"Hey, do you know which way to go?" I ask.

"I think so. I can find out." I hop back in the car. It's nice that he's doing this and not charging me. He drives around for a while, every turn is one-way, and we're on the wrong end, so he can't get around. Finally, he finds an entrance. I'm having a coughing fit and laughing while I talk about how silly it is I have to go to work when I sound like I have pneumonia. He's so kind. "Well, this will help me out too when I pick up or drop off other passengers. Now I'll know where to go."

So we're both helping each other tonight. He finds the entrance, and I hop out in my jeans and pink Converse sneakers.

"Thank you so much!" I close the door but run back.

"What's your name again?" I asked.

"Tarique!" He shouted.

"Tarique?" I asked.

"Tarique."

I'm spelling it that way because I'm not sure how to spell it. But he deserves the effort. He deserves to be known. All the people who go out of their way to help others in little situations that no one will ever know of deserve to be known.

I go into the hospital. I was really hoping it was just an Urgent Care Center and they could give me some medicine for this cough and fluid in my lungs, but hell, I'm in an emergency room. God fucking damn it. This is going to cost a lot. I have no insurance. All I wanted was some medicine.

I fill out my paperwork. I ask for a mask while I'm filling it out to be considerate to anyone else around my heaving. I saw a sign once in a hospital, I think in LA, that said, to ask for a mask if you were coughing to be considerate. I've been in so many damn hospitals, and this was all before the pandemic.

I remember my husband having a seizure because he drank so much water, just trying to stay hydrated while we rolled on some research chemicals in Sonoma, California. He drank so much water he lowered his sodium level, and he seized up. That was one of the worst days of my life. I heard something off in the other room. I saw him on the bed seizing. I thought he was overdosing. I lost it. I was so afraid, confused, and scared the love of my life was about to OD right there in front of me. I was so scared and confused that I slapped him in the face while he was having a seizure because I didn't know what to do, and I wanted him to wake up. I called the ambulance. It was a whole ordeal, and I'm traumatized to this day. He jokes about it, but I still don't think it's funny. Some of our young partying close calls have been funny but not that one. I'll never get over that one.

We always have the close calls that we laugh about. Usually, they are not mutual. Like, I'll laugh about the time I accidentally overdosed him on weed oil in our studio apartment in Hollywood and Cherokee back in LA.

When the paramedics came in, and literally, I'm serious, they LITERALLY said "If you can't do the time, don't do the crime."

That motherfucker literally said that. While my husband laid on the bed motionless, just so fucking high on weed, he thought he was dying. I laugh about that one. He doesn't. Because he thought he was dying.

Or the time I got so drunk years and years and years ago when we were much younger and much stupider. Less in love and more obsessed with each other. I had an episode and slit my wrist with his chef's knife right in the kitchen. Right there in front of him in the middle of a fight before either of us knew I was Bipolar and needed therapy and medication. Holy hell. I drank a whole bottle of Johnny Walker, waiting for him to get home. Because I knew he kissed a girl. Anyway. Back then, when I was clinically mentally ill, but didn't know it yet. Twenty-something, I didn't have grown ass woman conversations with my husband. I just drank a bottle of scotch.

"You want me sad? DO YOU WANT ME SAD? THIS IS ME SAD!" So I slit my wrists open in the kitchen with his chef's knife that he never cooked with again. He smacked me.

"WHAT THE FUCK HAVE YOU DONE?!"

Because he was so confused and so scared and so afraid, he didn't know what to do. The same way I slapped him when he was having a seizure back in Sonoma years ago. You just don't know sometimes. Sometimes you're just scared. He processed the shock quickly and realized he had to save me. Made a tourniquet, tied me up, and got me off the bloody slippery tile kitchen floor in Flatbush, Brooklyn.

"You have to call the ambulance. I'm going to bleed out." I moaned.

"You called the fucking ambulance, and you did this!"

I called the ambulance. They sewed me up and kept asking if I did it to myself, and I kept saying, "No no no. I was washing a beer glass, and it just cut me wide open!"

But I was still drunk and would get up trying to find him to make sure he was still there. To make sure he hadn't left his crazy ass partner there in the hospital. I found him in the waiting room.

"Ma'am, you have to go back to your bed and get stitched up."

"Okay. Okay," I said. I went back, and they stitched me up. Real ugly stitches. But I have a pretty tattoo over the scar now. It hurt like hell getting my sleeve tattooed over that scar tissue year and years and years later. But I guess I deserved that for ruining his expensive chef's knife.

But yeah. Hospitals. Been in a lot. So I filled out my paperwork and everything with my mask on. I have this medical ID card. I just hand doctors at this point so they can see I've had two heart surgeries, see I'm Bipolar, what medications I'm on, and such. It's all on my iPhone, and whenever I go in, just - click.

"Here ya go."

They're concerned about my coughing and feeling like there's fluid in my lungs, but they're more concerned with my heart rate.

"Your heart rate is too high for us to let you leave."

"I know, ma'am. I have tachycardia. I just came here because I have this feeling of fluid in my lungs when I cough."

I also let the doctor know I did some PCP earlier. At least he's happy I know the exact dose. I mean, at least he's met someone who does dissociative as safely as you can recreationally. "PCP? How much?"

"Exactly 42 milligrams about 4 hours ago, doc."

"How often do you do this?" The Doctor asked.

"Every day," I replied.

"You know it's not good for you, right?"

"Yes, I know." Well, neither is smoking cigarettes or drinking booze, or fucking too much, or I don't know. I would defend drugs up and down back then because I was on them. All of them. But I guess it's all relative. The best part about life is we don't know a goddamn thing about any of the rest of the people around us. And that's okay. We all just have to be kind to each other and don't lie to your doctor when you did a little PCP because he's just trying to do his job the best he can.

My nurse Philip, "Who are you? Get out of here. You look too healthy to be in my hospital."

Oh my god, he is the funniest motherfucker in this place.

"Cool converse. That's some old school." He says to me. He's weird and talks like a stand-up comedian, and I love it. I asked him what he likes to do. He says he likes trauma and ER and helping really sick people who really need help.

"So you don't like me?"

"Oh no. I like you! I like your personality! You're real! Everyone else comes in here crying over a stubbed toe or their girlfriends acting crazy."

(I used to be one of those crazy girlfriends) "I just wanted something for my lungs, man."

"I know. They're gonna make sure there are no fluids in there."

He likes my tattoos and tries to put a needle in the arm that's all colorful but then decides to go with the other arm. I tried to warn him. Not only are the tattoos in the way of that arm, but so is about a year of needle abuse. He glides over one of those machines nurses bring about the emergency room to patients with all our information saved on it.

"This computer is slower than my ex-girlfriend."

I fucking love you, Philip.

SIGNED, NOT LOVED

They scanned my lungs to see if there was any fluid in them. I've been here for hours now. This is not what I wanted to do tonight. They gave me a nice IV bag in my arm, which not only flushed away my high but made me have to piss really badly. But I don't want to use the emergency room bathroom because that's fucking gross. Another nurse came over, and there was no fluid in my lungs. I can buy something over the counter for the cough.

Are you fucking kidding me? Do you know how much a goddamn X-ray of my lungs is going to cost just to tell me I need DayQuil? And I have to use the emergency room bathroom because I won't make it home in time? I thought I had bronchitis or pneumonia or caught something terrible in Bolivia that was just now coming for me or something, anything, other than "an upper respiratory infection, otherwise known as the common cold." Well fuck.

Phillip is back!

He hands me my discharge papers.

"Here ya go. Sign your life away right here!"

I laugh.

"Ever heard that one before?"

This guy needs an award. I hop in an Uber back home. God damn it. More bills. Honestly, I would be madder, but Philip made my night. And I brought lavender hand sanitizer that I used all over after the emergency room bathroom.

My Husbands Footsteps

Here I lay this morning. Sprawled naked in the guest room. I moved here last night because I've been so sick I didn't want to wake the dogs or my husband with these coughing fits.

And I like this room more than the others. It's all white. White sheets.

White pillows.

White curtains.

White decor.

One gold pillow and a scratchy brown llama blanket from Peru.

I love closing the door. It's a small room, and I feel like I'm a world away when I lay on the fluffy comforter like a cloud but then get a little scratch from the llama underneath it.

The fire escape is just next to the bed, and I crawl out there sometimes for a cigarette.

It's beautiful. I love this city.

There's the door into the apartment where there's food and the couch and everything I own, and then my favorite door, the window, to the fire escape where I get to watch all the people walk by while I try not to ash on their little heads.

It just seems more peaceful in here. Anyway, the dogs followed me in. They follow me everywhere.

I love it.

They need me for some reason. I love it.

Still naked and crusty in the eyes, trying to determine how difficult work is going to be today based on the coughing fits.

SIGNED, NOT LOVED

I still feel sexy, though, which is nice. Naked, sick, and crusty-eyed.

I think it's special to still feel sexy when you're gross like that.

My husband is awake and noticed I'm not in bed with him. Which usually triggers his anxiety. PTSD back from the nights when I didn't come home at all. Which were the better nights? The worse ones were when the cops brought me home because they found me on the highway in LA naked, nothing on but ten-dollar heels and my two-thousand-dollar jacket missing.

Or a concerned pedestrian. Or he had to use my GPS location on my phone to find me blacked out in a bodega in Brooklyn a few blocks away from our apartment. Concerned cashiers were just trying to close their nice small business while my stupid drunk ass was trying to figure out where I lived. It wasn't far. They'd be on my phone with my dad and the cashiers, and then they'd hand my phone to my husband when he finally was able to locate me and brought me home.

Make sure I didn't break anything or beat on him. I usually beat on him, and he'd just call my dad, and then everyone would be sad because Rachael was black-out drunk again. My sisters would text me the next day and say, "I heard you're not feeling well. I love you." It meant the world to me but made me hate myself.

"I heard you're not feeling well" was an extremely kind choice of vocabulary. Dad would talk to me a couple of days later, telling me the next time I am going to kill myself or kill someone else, and have to live with that for the rest of my life. But it took a lot of nights of almost killing myself or killing someone else to make those nights stop happening.

I'm just glad I'm in the guest room. But he's still afraid.

Every time he wakes up, I'm not right there next to him. I feel terrible when I can hear his footsteps hurriedly checking the apartment. I hate that I've done that to him.

Not anymore.

61

But the damage is done.

"I need to go to the gym, but I want to spend time with you. I never see you," My husband said.

"But I want to write. I won't be paying attention to you anyway," I replied.

"But if I'm here, I'll want your attention. Because we never see each other, our schedules are so different."

"Well, that's what it's like living with a writer. I want to lock myself in this room for now because I finally feel inspired."

"YEAH? WELL, THEN, I'M WRITING A BOOK. A BOOK ABOUT WHAT IT'S LIKE TO LIVE WITH A WRITER. SO ALOOF AND NEVER WANTING TO LOVE ME."

He's honestly joking. He says it in his silly play voice we share together. A voice only he and I know, sometimes a language, words only he and I know. He flails his arms and hangs half his body off our dirty blue couch dramatizing everything to make sure I know he's playing.

I know he's joking. Because of our special voice, our secret language. But the words "you're so aloof and never wanting to love me" are a little more true than he knows, and this makes me sad. I do love him. To the depths of my soul, however far that is, his jokes are sometimes a bit too true. So I laugh and give him that smile I know he wants to see.

"Noodle, you know I love you so so much."

Just so he never catches on that our jokes, pokes, and sharp words are sometimes a bit more true on my end than his.

Depressed

The only way I can explain how I feel is that a monster inside me pulls at my consciousness and my physical being. She can make me do and think terribly dark things, but every step of the way, I'm playing tug of war. Sometimes I get exhausted and relinquish control which is when she takes over. For the past few days, I've let Her have me. I was too far gone to snatch back my heart from Her icy grasp. That bitch is strong.

I spent my whole day sleeping until the very second I had to leave for work. My poor dog, I'm the worst mother when She decides to fuck with me. I couldn't shower, it's been three days, and I was actually able to get in and wash myself today. The hot water seems to soothe Her appetite for destroying me just for a while.

The reason I know I'm at the tail end of this episode now is I'm writing this because I'm conscious, and I'm able to have my own thoughts. When I was deep in the abyss the past few days, I had no thoughts. I could function at the bare minimum, barely able to get to work. I think that's why people don't understand mental illness. We can talk about it and describe it until we are blue in the face, but can you comprehend your brain shutting off while you still have to exist in your physical body?

It feels like you are a marionette. You feel nothing. But you have to make every calculated move to physically control what you're doing. It takes an amount of energy I have no measurement for. When I was powerlifting, it took less energy than to move myself when I was depressed.

New York City

That city means the world to me.

I swear to God, and I found my soul in those streets.

I kicked pavement to the skyscrapers for the world to see.

Every block I walked hit a fiber in me.

Walking alone in Bed-Stuy.

Somewhere between sober and high.

There were so many faces.

Who the fuck was I?

So many people.

Too many things.

I started to give birth

To who I was supposed to be.

Glassy nights and busy sights started to uncork me.

My dad dropped his teenager off on a stoop

In a bad neighborhood.

Eight hundred in my bank account,

Nothing else but a dirty futon where we stood.

SIGNED, NOT LOVED

"I don't think this is a good idea."

He was right not to want me gone.

Me disappearing was always the same old song.

"I know you don't."

But no one has a choice once my mind is made.

He held me tight. When he cried, he looked away.

I have a way of needing to leave all the time.

And we had to pretend that I was going to be fine.

The air was heavy when he left that strange building.

Like something wasn't said by either of us

That wanted to escape.

Turns out that's just how it goes sometimes.

Turns out it's not all bedtime stories or fate.

Or is none of that true?

And we all just had to wait?

Way before you.

Way before we knew.

A young girl

Fighting the world alone.

Sometimes warm.

RACHAEL MADORI

Most times cold.

I wouldn't have done it anywhere else.

Life doesn't get easier,

I don't know if that helps.

I felt alive every time the subway shook me.

I remember that time you

"Took me"

Underneath the Brooklyn Bridge

"So quickly"

Just to show me where we were

And how we were

"So tiny."

Dropping acid in Central Park when it was snowy and too close to dark.

It was Christmas time.

Felt it in the air.

I could have happily died there.

I fell in love somewhere on 24th Street.

The city grew inside me once that happened.

"Hey, baby,

Order me an Old Fashioned?"

SIGNED, NOT LOVED

God.

I had love to ration.

It could have been the drugs.

It could have been the love.

Can I keep that feeling?

That city,

Every spot are little time capsules.

Raindrops hit the lights just like fractals.

No one but us seemed to like that weather.

We danced like fools in the rain together.

I think you and I have been crazy forever.

We would sit on the median and watch the traffic fly by.

You always laugh, and I always sigh.

Always watching people walk by.

We promised never to say goodbye.

I've dropped tears in the East River and the Hudson.

I laughed my way from Coney Island to Times Square.

Do you remember our spot in Dumbo?

Who we were was made there.

Hit By A Cab

One time I tried to beat a light in Manhattan and got hit by a Yellow Cab. It wasn't his fault.

But my foot was shattered, and to this day, I have an ugly bruise on my foot where it was destroyed.

I was disabled and thrown into months of depression and self-hatred for what I essentially did to myself.

I still think about that cab driver and how I ruined his night, day, or month.

But I guess I'm a real New Yorker now.

Living here for almost twelve years wasn't enough, but getting hit by a Yellow Cab was.

Why is my life always the hard way?

The medical bills, I can't say I know where they lay…

Andover, NJ 2020-ish

Silent Screams

He walked by me today. We didn't really catch eyes.

My heart hurt as he glided by.

Not even a glance towards my direction. Not a sigh.

Not a cry. Not a "Hi." Why?

Why. WHY!?

I felt a silent scream.

We're trapped in a silent fight.

Nothing get's said, which makes it all worse.

I'm in pain, but I don't think he knows how

I

Am suffocating.

Why can't he tell?

Or care?

Just pull me

Close.

We promised this wouldn't happen.

RACHAEL MADORI

I can't feel our love through the static.

Not like it used to be.

Not like it used to happen.

* * *

By the way,

We're in the same house. We live together

But don't talk.

I sleep in my own room. He in his.

No one ever told me this is what marriage is.

Broken Heart Whispers

I hold you up when your legs have become tired.

I whisper softly when the noises around you shatter like glass.

I breathe every breath in the hope to see a true smile come across your face.

And I know I am broken and damaged as well.

I fall down and fail the way human hearts do.

But I have been there before, and I have been thereafter.

One day I will not be there, or here, or anywhere.

It will be an acidic memory that strikes your gut and hazes your brain.

But I will not be there to whisper the loudness away.

Because you allow the voices to whisper to you, and there is no room for me.

And it is not that I do not have the strength to shout from the depths of my black lungs

To sanitize their filthy claws that clutch you.

It will be the strength that allows me to love myself with no footsteps beside me.

It will be a weakness,

It will be the lack of anything at all that allows you to hate yourself.

RACHAEL MADORI

My breath has become cold to preserve my tongue.

To preserve my sweet whispers to you in a jar,

On the shelf,

Because there is no room for me here.

Shine For You

The dense darkness in my mind never passed you by.

Past, present, and future are a cracked lens I peer through.

I'm a wild and sick enigma with good intentions gone awry.

Did I make the world difficult for you?

Sunset giggles settle on our lips, giving way to a fractal sky.

I dance for you in puddles, cleansing our journey to be reborn new.

I've shown you a life where I love to live and live to die.

Did I make the world magical for you?

Like a star that will burn if you're near but a gorgeous spectacle from below...

Like the twinkle of a blade before it punctures your heart through and through...

Like a beacon on the shore guiding you to safety against the ocean's flow...

I made this whole world shine for you.

RACHAEL MADORI

Heart Rape

I have been through hell.

But I have maintained my faith that the littlest

Bit of good in anyone evil is worth

The World.

And they deserve every chance to be loved

And allow that good to grow.

And I have been a bright light

Hidden.

Drunken

Somethings watching.

But always a light to the finish.

As I cry on these pages, I feel that light

Extinguish.

This darkness feels wrong. Like I'm just

Walking into a party.

Everyone stares.

I will be mean.

I will feel nothing.

SIGNED, NOT LOVED

I can feel nothing.

I will break hearts by mistake.

And flee here and there.

But the most curious thing about this;

Is it was not the molestation, the mental illness, the overdoses, the slit writs, the rapes, the gun to my head,

The guilt, the bodies - that finally gave space for the descent into the darkness to start.

Simply it was the heart.

I Deserve To Be Happy

I was not what they wanted since being in the womb.

Before I could go to the park, there sat on my childhood tomb. And so she moved on in a confusing whirl of fury and disregard. Only to look down at the scars realizing now I'm in charge.

At times, I still want to kick and scream like the child I never was. Sometimes I want to burn down the world just to find the cause.

But I sit with my rage, and I let her exist.

Because when the night is quiet and the bed empty, I am who I will always live with.

I deserve to be happier than ever.

I wish someone had told me sooner.

Ring

I threw my wedding rings into the Hudson. I don't wonder where the lay.

I barley remember the day.

RACHAEL MADORI

The End

Divorce was

The best

Self-care routine I've accomplished in 27 years.

The End…., The Beginning.

New York City, 2022-ish

Bed Sheets

There are things I am careful of owning.

Knives.

Guns.

Anything sharp?

Because I'm sick sometimes.

Or all the time.

But the last time,

The bed sheets in July.

I can't not have bed sheets.

But I tied them around my staircase

And asked YouTube how to make a noose.

Then I hung myself.

I fell and cried.

Tried again.

Did I really need to die?

RACHAEL MADORI

I called the hotline.

The police took me away again and locked me up.

I lied and lied and got released.

My neck still sore,

I went to work.

And no one knew.

And still don't.

It's difficult, you know.

To listen to your boss complain

When you weaponized bed sheets 24 hours ago.

Dido

My family doesn't want me to drink anymore. My therapist doesn't want me to drink anymore.

My AA meeting doesn't want me to drink anymore. I don't want to drink anymore.

But sometimes, when I'm lonely, the scotch is warm.

And sometimes, when I think about the taste of my grandfather's tongue down my throat,

The vodka burns my mouth just right.

I Can't Seem To Find

There's a song that was the soundtrack to my life when I was houseless and on drugs.

It was my song at the strip club.

It was on in the car while we drove around and did what we did.

I would listen to it high.

I haven't heard it in years, and it just randomly showed up in a Tik-Tok video.

My heart started to race.

The memories started to violate me.

I started to drool.

I got horny.

I could feel a needle slide inside me.

I turned up my phone,

Hugged it close to my ear until the volume hurt my eardrum.

I moaned.

Turned it on my speaker.

Held it close.

Let the goosebumps roll over me.

I got nauseous, like I actually just shot up.

I whined in my bed for a moment until I snapped out of it.

It's been ten fucking years since that time, and still,

This.

FBI

"Just updating you, he was found guilty." The text bubble pops up on my phone.

I sigh in relief,

As if,

It makes,

Any difference that the man,

Who the FBI investigated for using me in CP,

Was found guilty.

I offered them tea when they first came to my new apartment after the divorce.

"Would you like some tea? Could I see your badges again?"

They gave me the report to read,

I threw up in the toilet.

"Forgive me."

The woman agent looked at me first, "It's alright." The male agent stayed quiet the entire interview. I enjoyed that.

I saved her number.

I text her sometimes.

Collection #122522

Yum

The beat in my heart is livid.

The pulse in my veins is not timid.

I curl my toes in ecstasy

Even though

Nothing is happening to me.

I want to bite.

I want to fight.

I want to carry the light.

Craving a petite woman.

Not to harm her,

Well, not in a way that she wouldn't like.

SIGNED, NOT LOVED

Lips wet for innocence.

Legs are too long to take a lick.

I think her blonde hair would taste better in between my teeth.

I can't tell if it's a monster inside me

Or if it's just me all underneath.

RACHAEL MADORI

The Grim Reaper Turns Me On

Does Death fascinate me because when it finally wraps me in its arms,

Something in my mind will finally have certainty.

Finally, the ups and downs will find their way home.

When Death finds me,

Finally, I will not be alone.

Living Dead Girl

Stuck in this limbo.

With or without.

I am the scaffolding.

I am the bones.

A human being,

Robbed of a soul.

But she'll come back.

Swim to the brink.

Through the sea of the dead.

She will come qualm

The voices in my head.

When I felt my peachy flesh

On the hangman's noose

Tighten…

I was simply looking

For the peace that she provided.

A treacherous path.

Where the only people I seem to meet

RACHAEL MADORI

Are caricatures of me.

No one seems to see,

I am not free.

I am screaming.

I am pleading.

I am not on my knees.

I am not yielding.

Stuck in this limbo.

With or without.

I am tearing at my skin.

I am begging to be let out.

I live somewhere in the clouds

And somewhere under the ground.

Life of the undead is a life unlike any other.

It is solitary.

It is cold.

There are bones in the river.

I will never be found.

One day when I am dead in the ground,

do not weep.

SIGNED, NOT LOVED

Do not make a sound.

It is the Quiet

I have finally found.

Rape

I'm going to make a piece about rape

Because if I don't

It's not fair,

If it's not in a line,

It doesn't do justice to my fate.

I'll talk about a lot of shit and just spit with hate.

Not hate that I hold onto here,

Because I'm clear and I overcame what YOU did "my dear."

I think the details are less to talk about it's more about the amount.

So let's start off with number one.

What a son of a gun.

He took me to the back, behind a Taco Bell and said

"You're my girlfriend, this is just what you're supposed to do."

I was Young, naive, didn't have a clue.

Am I lucky because he didn't fuck me but just forced his dick down my throat.

Why I was so trusting?

Number two, sometimes I lose count.

Same guy, bedroom, closed door, shushed room.

SIGNED, NOT LOVED

I was signed out of sex-ed so I had no clue what a dick or a pussy looked like to me or to you.

He pushed me down.

I was so fucking confused like "What the hell are you going to do?"

"Be quiet. Don't move. This might hurt."

Looking down.

Jeans get pulled down.

Fourteen, I don't know shit about what's about to go down.

All I know is he's doing what he's doing and I had no knowledge, no teaching, and no nothing.

Just remember a preacher preaching that this isn't right but in the moment there was nothing.

* * *

Move on to number three.

This time still in my teens, when my boss thinks he can have the last word dangling your job in front of you.

"Fuck me in my office."

I listened.

How about number four with the guy that ran the drugs with me and raped me when I was high.

OD-ed on a couch, in a blur, passing in out and out until I woke from a black out.

Dick in me and him just using my body like I wasn't somebody.

"Oh, I'm so sorry I just thought you were sleeping"

Bitch you know what you were doing.

I'm no sleeping beauty.

You don't get to just go and use me.

But you did.

And I tried to run you over with my car.

That I'll never forget.

And it goes and goes, there's been tolls unpaid on the road, in my past too many men to count, trying to take me out for the count.

Lock me in a room in the strip club.

Saying "this is just what you have to do" tell the DJ turn the bass up

So no one hears me scream beneath the damn booth when the bass drops.

They always say something like "this is what you have to do."

If you're told that from a young age

SIGNED, NOT LOVED

To always listen to men

To always obey

To always submit

Well perhaps,

I can blame that.

* * *

RACHAEL MADORI

Or blame them.

Who's to say?

Because it keeps happening.

Even in my grown up job.

With my grown up mind.

I went to her house

Thinking I made friends.

But it was all a lie.

A dinner party only to be disrupted

By someone I trusted.

She reached down my shirt

And asked me to fuck her and her husband.

I said no.

Which should have been enough.

But she grabbed me again at my pants

And I was outnumbered.

However this time, I am older and have had the tolls stolen too many times.

So I grabbed her by the throat and pulled her off me.

Drank the rest of their wine and let myself out of the apartment free.

Walking through the West Village.

SIGNED, NOT LOVED

Just crying.

I can't help but feel

Like everyone

Is out

To get me.

Another Gin Whisper

I stood on the corner in the cold.

Bounced my head off the cement wall.

Cigarette hanging off my red lip didn't fall.

Why can't my legs just keep walking?

I head into the bar.

"Don't go in you fucking idiot." Voice 1 screams.

"Good girl. My good little bitch." Voice 2 gleams.

I'm honestly not even mad at myself right now.

Yeah. Fuck you voices, tonight I know you won.

I'm lucky I got home

And just had one.

"Gin martini. Up. Twist. Thanks."

I can't tell if this is anger

Or complacency.

Can't wait to get home

And smash the mirror at what I see.

I wonder if people who struggle get the tears when they read what I say.

SIGNED, NOT LOVED

I wonder if it makes you feel better that I'm right here on the dark roads that we roam.

I wonder if it calms your shakes when you know that you're not alone.

But today it got a piece of me.

I gave it away like a cheap date.

It's insane that someone can live with this much hate.

It's crazy because I still love myself.

No matter how much I slip and swerve.

I still know what I deserve.

I guess if I let it make me hate myself I would have jumped off the bridge by now.

And I still love myself even when the cool gin hits my red lip.

I still convince myself I'm a good person

With every sip.

Maybe if God was as persistent

Satan wouldn't have shown.

But He doesn't. Or maybe He's a bit more subtle.

RACHAEL MADORI

Maybe He's my husband holding me crying or my dad calling me every night making sure I'm sober.

Well He doesn't know shit about the score board because the Devil straight up invites Himself over.

And we drink and we fuck and things are generally normal.

I tie Him up but He begs to be let loose so we take a stroll.

And I think I have Him at bay

But the whole time He has control.

Live a life of close calls.

I was never the kid you could let loose.

Find me on top of the world or find me in a noose.

I've made peace with it.

I don't think my family ever will.
Hold still.
Hold still.

No in between.
Extremes.
Only.
So.
You,

As fucking lonely?

She's Out!

She's out.

She's manic.

But let's not panic.

I've been waiting for the day.

Been waiting for the wave.

The wave up is louder,

Than the wave down encounter.

The Dark Woman there is evil.

But this ones got her own crown.

Today she's vibrant

And feral.

I better be careful.

I'm torn between these women who I am.

But if They're both me, where do I stand?

Damn!

RACHAEL MADORI

I feel pretty.

…What is with me?

Two weeks ago

I was at my wrists,

Slitting.

This Bipolar,

She's a tight holder.

Sometimes she's outta ammo.

Right now

One's in the holster.

Today it's loaded.

I feel it in my throat.

mmmmmmmmmm.

* * *

SIGNED, NOT LOVED

Gotta keep composure.

Don't let the monsters closer.

I'm stronger than the both of them.

Keep Them in Their cages,

Rattling.

Soon I'll be sad again.

Then I'll be mad at them.

They can't keep their shit together.

But truth is,

I am Them.

Men

Men,

Such fragile creatures.

My husband can't even make eye contact with our Chihuahua while I give him a sloppy blow job without being traumatized.

My hoop earrings bouncing while I do what I do with my throat.

Now I am not getting laid.

He is playing video games. I'm weighing out the drugs.

Good thing I also have a boyfriend, a therapist I'm trying to fuck, and a very, very good Hitachi Magic Wand for myself.

At least being a pornstar taught me how to pleasure myself indulgently, without the need for men.

Being such fragile creatures they are.

A Vessel

A vessel

A vessel

I feel like a vessel.

I tip. I swish. I pour.

All to drown in tears on the floor.

Just to perk back up, normal.

Normal? I can't tell you what's normal.

They pour what they want in.

A vessel.

I react because I'm at their whim.

I wish I could shatter into pieces

So the emotions would disappear.

But the only thing holding me together

Is the fact that they're here.

I've stopped my medication abruptly.

I can no longer let those pills suck me.

And it's dangerous but

Fuck, fuck, FUCK ME.

I need to be me again. In place again. Safe again. Alive again.

All of this is getting quite frightening.

But if I am meant to feel then I am done running away

Or trying to medicate.

Being numb is making it impossible to reciprocate.

I can't believe they make people live in this state.

I'll say it again and ten times over, shouting the farthest.

 I could be safe, chemically induced.

But I'd very much rather just be a dead artist.

Life and death don't scare me.

It's what I allow myself to be while still here.

As far as I'm concerned I'm alive.

But I am also dead.

So there's really nothing to fear,

Except what goes on in my head.

Baby, They'll Kill You Too

There's a few different people inside of my head.
I'm convinced most of them want me dead.

You keep loving my brokenness
Right on cue.
Baby please,
They will kill you too.

There's no need for more casualties.
You need to get away from me.
I won't survive if our story ends.
But these voices are my only friends.

Remember that time I wanted to jump in the Hudson?
That water feeling me up would have been something.
Why does it feel so right if it's actually wrong?
I know you keep calling me home,
but I'm already gone.

There's no need for more casualties.

RACHAEL MADORI

You need to get away from me.

I won't survive if our story ends.

But these voices are my only friends.

Your eyes are my medicine.

What am I supposed to do when my demons start creeping in?

I know you want to be my hero and make it in the end.

But these voices,

They are truly my only friends.

Take Me

Rape me.

Date me.

Text me.

None of it matters if you see

What they do to me

What they say to me.

What they see is not what I see.

Another use, abuse, excuse.

What is your use?

What are you good for?

I know you wanted more.

Whore.

I'll take you, make you, break you.

If you let me, there will be no more "You."

Let it ensue.

You had no clue

That we took you

And mistook you.

Know we will not stop until we're through.

We will take it.

All of you.

Stand true.

They cannot take the "Who."

Perhaps, the why, where, and when

Because they think they can take all of you.

But underneath, they had no clue.

That "Who"

Was You.

They're screwed.

You

You are here.

It is amazing

That from all of the darkness,

All of the fear

You made it here.

Rejoice in yourself,

The good and the bad.

Because without either

And both

A different you we would have.

And she is fantastic in her own sphere.

But it is You that I want here.

I Always Have To Go

I love you.

But I hate you.

Because you show me comfort and

Love that I have never known.

You give me a world that is safe,

However

I am only happy when I am unknown.

To be alone.

To let my heart break

Is worth everything

To experience life at its peak.

Pain is pleasure

And just for good measure,

I'll stretch out my leisure,

Find another girl to please her.

I'm the bad guy.

SIGNED, NOT LOVED

Or bad girl.

I don't like gender.

I don't belong in this world.

Who knows?

Where we go?

When we slow?

Where the planets grow?

What did I sow?

How did you know?

Here I go.

Give me the show.

 It's time I knew what I'm supposed to know.

There I go.

Small Princess

You are a small princess.

Or so you've been told.

Not princess enough for someone to hold.

At times too timid.

At times too bold.

You are alone, small princess.

You will learn to survive this way.

You will make them leave when they want to stay.

This is the way.

You will be safe.

Because no one showed you the way.

How did you land on this planet, and no one else knows?

How could anyone, small princess, let you go?

Your mind scared them.

Ensnared them.

They cannot see

SIGNED, NOT LOVED

What I see.

Oh.

To be seen.

Not Another Suicide Fantasy

The deepest feeling,

Beyond the gut or soul

Is knowing that you will take your own life,

And you know exactly the toll.

That you will end your breath,

No matter how long they say, you have left.

A show, a concert, life puts on.

But you know what may happen after every song.

When will the voices cease?

One day you will hate it,

But I will find peace.

Peace.

Don't speak my name.

Leave.

To disappear

Piece

By

Piece.

The Monsters in My Bedtime Stories

I remember when my dad would tell me bedtime stories.

Back in the day, when I had no worries.

Back when I thought it'd be like that forever

With his face in my nightlight.

Back when I thought his arms would protect me

My whole life.

And life keeps moving along

To a never-ending sound.

Please tell him I was wrong.

Don't know what its worth

Til I'm in the ground.

When I was young, there were wars being waged in my soul.

I would take a hit in my veins

Just to ease the toll.

But what's running from my monsters ever done for me?

Except make darkness

The only thing I see.

Now I keep it moving. Keep pushing. Keep playing.

RACHAEL MADORI

If I'm fighting demons, might as well be slaying.

Maybe when I'm older it won't hurt to feel.

All I know is the monsters in his stories were real.

Dead and Golden

It was not long into childhood

When I lost all I had known.

Before a little girl went places,

A little girl should never go.

I had a good eight years before the monsters and pain.

I guess almost ten years of innocence isn't enough to buy you through the whole game.

And slowly, at the hand of men, society, and her own will that had wilted, her roots became weak ad her true soul stilted.

The roses' petals drooped, and no matter the cries,

Not a soul extended a hand.

So down went the rose, bruised and weak.

Unable to stand.

But eventually, a miraculous hand came to the roses' aid.

And she took a moment to take in the soil of suffering in which she laid.

And within a moment, the touch of this familiar hand lit the flower until white smoke rose.

RACHAEL MADORI

With all its bruises, bends, and falls easy to see,

The precious Rose dripped in gold.

An eternal reminder that the most beautiful things

Are only beautiful

On our own accord.

Boring Voices

Fuck.

I did it again, just like we all do.

"Are you okay?"

"Yeah. I'm okay."

"Are you okay, too?"

But we're both lying,

Or we don't care.

Just some more words to fill up the air.

I just don't need the worry and the inconvenience.

For someone to care and try to fix all of this shit.

I'll just keep moving on with the rest of the cloudy mist.

Staring violently at what's pumping beneath my wrist.

"Just do it already; everyone is waiting."

"Not right now, guys. I really don't feel like playing."

At least, that's how I talk to the voices soaring.

Cause sometimes they just get so fucking boring.

119

Rage

Rage.

Rage is all my little body feels.

Rage all done up behind tightly pulled back hair.

Rage stuffed up in a suit.

Rage behind red lipstick.

Rage in my heels when I stomp.

Like a little fish in a fish bowl.

They all watch.

They're all watching.

The people.

The not people.

Watching.

The people ask, "Are you okay?"

The not people just nod.

Because they understand.

I smile, crazy.

Like the Cheshire Cat.

Everything fades away.

But my pinned-up smile stays.

SIGNED, NOT LOVED

Stuck.

Because that's what they want to see.

Because they can't handle the fierce.

They need a pretty smile.

A smile I want to cover with blood.

Pull up through my gums.

Show my teeth.

There's a smile.

No one understands the angry fish.

I just let them watch and worry.

"How did she just switch?"

"Hey, you're scaring me."

 I'm scaring you?

Imagine how I feel.

I want to be with the not people.

In a dimension with things that understand the crazy.

When I rip off my clothes.

Tear down my hair.

Scream.

Cry.

Hit the windshield.

Hit the mirror.

But I am calm.

This is calm for the people.

The people don't know what it feels like to not be a person.

They care.

But they don't know.

They hurt themselves by caring.

I hurt them by them caring.

But they don't know.

The monster takes over.

She feels good.

The not people like Her.

She is like them.

She likes blood like them.

Little angry fish in a fish bowl.

Under a magnifying glass.

Being watched.

Like an animal.

Like an experiment.

Like a study.

* * *

RACHAEL MADORI

I'll break out.

Shatter the glass.

Be free.

With me.

With all of the me.

We'll be free.

With nothing more for the people.

And everything for the not people to see.

My Reflection

Sitting on cold ground, I hear all the thoughts I fear.

Maybe I should be buried deep down under here.

I bring you the burden

And chaos

And after that

More.

Keep fighting these fights.

But what is it really all for?

My reflection, my enemy.

My eyes will continue to hide.

When I look at my body, I see that there's no one inside.

My mind, the voices, they love for me to sing them a song.

Too bad.

I'm already gone.

Stop trying to help.

In the end, it will only hurt you.

I'm up in flames.

Don't get burned by me too.

RACHAEL MADORI

I'm sick and tired of riding this wave each day up and down.

Please, God, let me go before I fall off and drown.

My reflection, my enemy. My eyes will continue to hide.

When I look at my body, I see that there's no one inside.

My mind, the voices, they love for me to sing them a song.

Too bad.

I'm already gone.

* * *

SIGNED, NOT LOVED

Here we go.

I'm not surprised anymore.

Tired of hiding and running.

My bones are all broken and sore.

It's been up for auction, and now my soul has been sold.

This can't be hell because my eyes and skin are so cold.

My reflection, my enemy. My eyes will continue to hide.

When I look at my body, I see that there's no one inside.

My mind, the voices, they love for me to sing them a song.

Too bad.

We're already gone.

You're My Dinner

Men.

Men have caused me nothing but trouble.

But I love trouble.

Although they're evil and prey.

I keep my hands on the wheel and pray.

They can't make me leave.

I will stay.

I'm not a toy anymore.

Though they try and play.

I'll eat them alive.

Baby, get on my plate.

You're my dinner.

You're a sinner.

I'm a winner.

I'm a sinner, too, but the Devil is scared.

Because He wants me but can't have me.

Like the rest of them.

No one can have me.

SIGNED, NOT LOVED

Can't own me.

Can't throw me.

Can't push me.

Can't pull me.

I am me.

I am mine.

All this learned with bruised fists and time.

I'm not yours. You're mine.

I'll rhyme, I'll cry, I'll find peace and die.

But until then, I'll fight.

I'll bite.

I'll be wrong, and I'll be right.

But to those little girls who are not sure, not yet, not quite.

Fight.

Keep your fist and glare tight.

Keep your head in wonder and your dreams in sight.

The Devil and the men are thieves.

But you've got you, and you've got me.

We'll make them see.

We'll make them bleed.

Just like they did to you.

RACHAEL MADORI

Lock them in a cage.

The animals, you don't feed.

Breathe, girl.

Let it be.

Let it be.

Open your eyes.

They can't see what we see.

A Whole Load of Emotion

Brooklyn air is sticky, humid, and suffocating.

The icy breath of the subway doors opening makes me jump in.

Like I jumped in the pool at my Babci's house.

Just to cool off.

I love all the faces of people on subways.

I like that in every seat,

Every firm stance holding onto silver bars,

There is a story up in their heads.

Whether they're on their phones,

Like I am right now,

Or looking around listening to music…

I want to know where they are going.

How they are feeling.

What has their day been like?

I want to know their struggles,

Pain

Sorrow

Happy

131

RACHAEL MADORI

Disgust

Mistakes

Accomplishments.

I don't know why

I need to know and feel,

All of these things

From all of these strangers.

I feel like I want to let them know how important they are.

That they'll make it.

That they're doing their best.

Or maybe not

And that they should.

Why do I care?

So much so that I even write about it

And stare at them as they wobble on the subway.

I ache to know what they feel,

Which is ridiculous because I have enough shit going on in my own soul.

SIGNED, NOT LOVED

I feel like a vacuum that just wants all the emotions, waves, vibes and flow.

Just sucking it all up and swallowing it like a huge load.

I just love emotion.

I just fucking love them.

Memories on LSD

Memories.

Memories when I'm on that LSD.

Daddy's home. Daddy's home.

Don't trip up the patio.

So many girls just running round having fun.

So many littles girls don't know how the rent gets done.

My sister.

My sister, did I miss her?

She's always with Cassie.

She always looks past me!

Barbecues and tattoos.

Daddy just knocked Scott's lights out.

Scott's a bad man, but daddy's got us.

Me and mommy wait for the school bus.

Now looking at palm trees and mountains.

In LA a grown woman away.

SIGNED, NOT LOVED

Trying to clear all of my sins.

I can drink this wine

I can whine all night,

But I won't shy from where I came from.

Cause I'm the only one who gets shit done.

Make People, Plastic Masks

Can you hear me now?

The story I've been telling my whole life.

I'll follow my performance with a bow.

They always told me I have to play nice.

Wake up.

Pick a mask.

Pour breakfast in a flask.

Stay numb.

Smile and wave.

Just another happy day.

I hate all their plastic faces.

The kind of bullshit everyone in a room can see.

Stop pretending that you're going places.

You can't contour your personality.

Wake up.

Pick a mask.

Pour breakfast in a flask.

SIGNED, NOT LOVED

Stay numb.

Smile and wave.

Just another happy day.

I can't wear that face no more.

I don't have time for games, plays, charades and lying.

I can see past your fake allure.

Behind every single mask - we're crying.

RACHAEL MADORI

The Dogs Don't Think I'm Crazy

I don't think I'm crazy.

I'm glad my doctor didn't suffocate me.

I don't like the meds,

But at least they regulate me.

But maybe I am crazy.

Maybe when the dogs run around crying, whining and barking

It's not towards the rats, roaches or thunder.

Sometimes I think the dogs see something other.

But I feel strong and I feel like I'm fire.

I feel like I'm an opponent.

I feel like I'm dire.

I feel like I'm a fighter.

But I can never see my fellow contester.

Ghost Love

She posted a photo today.

Why not one of her face?

Why not show off some grace?

I don't understand what I felt.

Some type of longing, aching, regret I've been dealt.

But she was never truly mine.

A sister in friendship.

By time, skewed in my mind.

Obviously, never in her hazel eyes.

I lived in her house.

She showed me LA.

We'd play music loud

In the car

Just to go to the bank.

RACHAEL MADORI

I remember her plumped lipped smile.

That fucking attitude

Her sexy style.

Everything,

All of her,

It drove me wild.

I wonder about her sometimes,

If she filled in that tattoo on her inner left arm.

The one time I dragged her from the car

When I thought she took her life.

When we first met she had this earth energy that almost couldn't keep me away.

But something strange happened. Something I couldn't explain, something,

Very LA.

We had great years. We dried painful tears.

We shared deepest fears.

Then one day she disappeared.

Like a beautiful ghost with much better things to do.

Which I understand, because I abandon people too.

SIGNED, NOT LOVED

That pains me even more when I think about her.

Reminding me that we are somewhat similar.

MANIAC

I can tell I'm manic when I start to act like I did years ago,

It brings me back to days of running drugs.

Stripping.

Fast.

Fast.

Paced.

Moving.

Sliding.

Hiding.

Put the knife under your sleeve, lie.

I've been lying.

Little ones that mean nothing in the grand scheme of things but they're lies.

That crack head I made "friends" with when he snatched my phone.

I ran through Paterson trying to get it back.

Shooting up my veins in shopping mall parking lots.

Doing lines on my dashboard just to get by.

That's all real.

But she tells tall tales and spins it deeper.

Makes a fantasy that I was there or wasn't there.

Ah shit LET HER OUT.

I think She wants to be locked up because She deserves it for the people She hurt.

SIGNED, NOT LOVED

The people She killed.

The families She affected.

Yeah.

Take it slow.

I don't roll like that anymore.

These other dimensions I'm in.

Not safe.

Not safe for my husband.

I caught this maniac quick.

I want to lock myself in my room so I don't go out to fabricate and compensate.

Remember the real you.

They dragged along, just for the high and run the game for your fix,

You.

You always wanted to be a Queen.

I'm a Queen now, my new life my success.

But this maniac in my brain wants me back on the memories of the vein.

I'm out. I'm out.

I take the last train.

Away from the pain.

Outta the rain.

Rest in peace to the slain.

Hang on to what I've built.

Fuck.

Like being on a fucking stilt.

Bipolar Roller

I am so empty.

It was better when I felt nothing.

Nothing is better than this.

This is pain.

This is unrelenting suffering.

The memory of happiness makes it more painful.

The fact I know things used to be normal is excruciating.

I feel like I'm on a rollercoaster that's winding, pushing and pulling.

The motion sickness kicks in as I realize this is my life forever.

My mind is a ride that I'm trapped in forever.

My seat is my coffin.

I'm a prisoner to which way the wind blows.

It is my favorite ride when I'm up high

Death is the only way out when I'm low.

Everyone watches from the outside.

Everyone on the ground can't see what's happening to me.

How sick this ride is making me.

Their faces spin and twirl as I watch them live a normal life below.

RACHAEL MADORI

Strapped in.

Locked in.

No one listens to my cries to let me out.

How am I not used to this yet?

Spin, hang on, spin, hold tight, spin.

"Just let go."

Why can't I just let go?

Because I'm praying to go up again.

BIRTHDAY

Let me tell you something about my birthday.

Let me yell through punching the mirror at my face.

No, wait, I'm better now and the crazy is gone.

Yeah right, "I'm better now"?

My peace is only from dusk to dawn.

I don't pull my hair out.

I don't slit my wrists.

I don't jump on my building roof throwing fits.

I don't lie to my doctor when he thinks that they're working.

The meds, I mistakenly miss.

He wants to call me the proof.

The proof that the meds make me not want to be on the roof.

This is why my birthday is a particular day for me.

Every year it's a date I'm not supposed to see.

So when it comes around I hold it near.

Because birthdays don't last forever.

Like all beautiful things, they disappear.

RACHAEL MADORI

Motherfuckers hate when I say that too.

"Oh stop that talk, that'll never happen. We love you!"

To anyone else those may sound like genuine words to choose,

But let's take a moment to be in my bloody shoes:

You take my pain, suffering, instability, fear and paranoia just to boo hoo.

Make a fool out of all my screws that are loose.

Twist them back in me and make it all about YOU?

Let's say I can never leave because you'll cry or be hurt.

Let's make this about you until I'm dead in the dirt.

* * *

SIGNED, NOT LOVED

You think the demons and horrors I'm fighting

Aren't something I gear up for every day?

You think if they got me on my death day

I would even have a fucking thing to say?

I don't know if it works but I pray.

I don't know if it works but I stay.

I don't know if I am but sometimes I feel like prey.

I don't know if I am but sometimes I can't keep It at bay.

But my birthday is something It can't take away.

Nine-thousand eight hundred and sixty-two days as my pencil hits right now.

To be honest, people suffering out here popping pills sometimes ask me…

"How?"

I say lame brained things like "hope, love, family and medical help".

Truth is, for twenty-seven years I didn't know then and I don't know now.

Truth is, for twenty-seven years a part of me is grasping at heaven,

Peaked it once or twice,

But mostly most likely,

I like to live in hell.

Not even here.

RACHAEL MADORI

Not even on this plain.

I'm surprised if any of you even know my name.

The voices think that's absolutely insane.

I don't think they like me anymore.

They don't like how much I like to play their game.

PSYCHO TASTING MENU

Course 1

Brooklyn Tap Water

Paired with DEPAKOTE 250MG anti-psychotic medication

Course 2

5 Cheese Perogies

Course 3

68mg of PCP

Course 4

Cup of Turmeric tea with honey

Palette Cleanser

Brush your teeth

One lick of Vanilla Beeswax Chapstick Bottle of water under the bed for the evening

 I should be dead.

RACHAEL MADORI

People Like You More When You Kill Yourself

I laugh until I cry.

Post these photos for the likes.

Everything looks so good,

Even when I tell them it's really not.

I guess that's what happens when no one cares

Because that's just what they're taught.

I keep smiling in every photo.

Even though inside I'm saying "oh, no".

Because one day my gleam will dull.

All the likes and smiling faces

Will bitch and moan at the funeral.

They'll say "oh I just can't imagine"

and "she was just so beautiful".

But I'm just like the last one

and the very next to come.

Filling people's cups and then more

Until I realize mine was about to spill.

They'll all say they "just can't believe it".

When they might as well of handed me the fucking pill.

So keep it moving girl, keep it shaking.

All of us are asleep as much as we want to think we're waking.

Scaffolding

Like a skeleton hanging in a classroom.

Like an empty loft with a draft blowing through the ceiling beams.

Like the shed skin of a snake drifting on the sand.

I can remember feelings and emotions.

I recall I was a person with a soul before.

But right now she is gone, it is just scaffolding.

Right now there is a breeze through my chest,

Emptiness in my gut and hollow in my soul.

It's cold in here.

Humans seem strange, the way their faces move and shape with emotion.

I used to be like that.

I will be like that again.

I will be bubbly, bright, loving and filled to the brim with emotions and empathy.

I'll be a fully bloomed garden, a wild and alive forest.

But for now I am nothing but frame work.

I am the structure that keeps me tall and standing.

And I will find relief when she comes back to fill up all the space she's left vacant for now.

I don't know where she goes.

Perhaps so much emotion cannot exist for too long.

So she has to sneak away when I'm not looking to take a break.

It is my job to hold things up until she comes back.

Fire Escape Pussy

I climb out onto my dirty fire escape

To light up a cigarette.

Wearing only a thin shirt, red slides on my feet and black panties.

I wonder if anyone walking by can see my underwear.

A nice lady pushes her slushie cart below me.

I make sure not to ash on her, I know she's just trying to make some money.

A gentleman dressed nicely carrying a bag

Passes by in the other direction

With big headphones on

rushing to work.

I wonder what he's listening to.

I remember I'm on my period and don't have anything sanitary on.

I hope nothing red

Drips down my leg.

That would be worse than ashing on someones little head.

Plus it would ruin my white sheets

As I climb back through the window

Onto the bed.

RACHAEL MADORI

Daj Mi Buzi

Daj

mi

buzi.

Daj

…mi

…buzi.

I whisper these words softly to myself.

Alone on the couch. Memories swiftly kiss my brain.

This comfy, soft, familiarity rolls across my tongue like cotton.

I remember a scratchy wet kiss on my cheek.

Her grey hairs smushed against my face.

The memories are so vague.

I clutch it like a dove.

Though I feel I may pop its eyes out

Just to hold it a bit longer.

Pure love.

A Babci.

SIGNED, NOT LOVED

Squeezing her grandchild.

I will never

Have that pleasure again.

A Throne

"I can't tell if I'm on a downswing.

Because I don't feel depressing.

This makes me fear She will come out.

The other one.

Mania.

I'm in this red lull.

I sit on my throne.

Am I comfortable?

I feel in control.

But I don't want to be a fool.

I feel like I'm in a red room.

I actually feel pretty cool.

There it is.

There's the rule.

There's the hint

Of something other in control.

SIGNED, NOT LOVED

And that's how I roll.

To find out the temperature.

The temp is hot.

The voices mild.

But me, I feel wild.

Ah, so there She is.

It' been a while.

A bit more bitey.

 A bit more fighty.

I'm on this throne,

Watching her.

Just in case She gets feisty.

Here She is.

Awake and ready to be known.

Let's sit Her down.

She can look up at me on my throne.

RACHAEL MADORI

I know you're here. I know your moves.

The pyscho inside me - She stands up smooth

She seems complacent. Has She been abused?

No. Not abused, Just trained.

If She's going to make my life hell She knows She'll be restrained.

It's okay baby, You're my favorite me.

But I make the choices in this disease.

So we can continue this conversation

But I'm on point and You know your station.

My wild lover. Feral, sexy and free.

I'm the only reason You exist

So You don't make moves without me.

When the Lights Go Out

When the lights go out I feel like something is watching me.

From all corners of the house, every noise produces eyes.

It's outside.

It's inside.

If I close my eyes to sleep it's standing above me.

I'm in a constant state of fear until the morning comes or I count myself to sleep.

But counting doesn't always work.

Like it knows I'm trying to avoid thinking about it or feeling it stare at me.

The drugs will make the paranoia stop so I know It's not real.

Am I hearing voices? Whispers?

But if it's not real, why is my heart racing and why am I jumping at every sound?

I can only keep my eyes closed for a second

Because I feel like as soon as I open them it will be right on top of me.

RACHAEL MADORI

I don't care.

I just want to lay in peace.

Is everyone this terrified to go to sleep?

I cannot trust my brain.

I cannot trust my brain.

I cannot trust my brain.

I cannot trust my brain.

I cannot trust my brain.

I cannot trust my brain.

I cannot trust my brain.

I cannot trust my brain.

Can Only Speak In Poetry These Days

I am living in this being of darkness.

The pain is drunken and sporadic.

I live in pain.

There is another power at play.

I must turn this into a game,

Or it will make me insane.

I am choking.

The words can't be spoken.

I am fluid.

My being is liquid.

I move and flow with emotion

Like the ocean.

The current is unsure and unspoken.

I dive deep into the field of emotion.

In search of the purest evil inside me,

The verboten.

RACHAEL MADORI

The Building is on Fire

Visiting home is like running into a burning building.

There's fire, there's bodies, the kind you can't see, as I breathe in the memories.

My grown up fingers burn as I touch the places I used to be.

"It couldn't have been all bad" I let myself know.

But it's hard to recall anything other than suffering in the garden in which they expected me to grow.

The forest I assumed would calm my childhood nerves.

But the deeper I Lear into my backyard my heart begs to sob.

Bracing for the memories of laying in the leaves with a .45 down my throat at seventeen.

Just like all my cheap blow jobs.

That leads my mind down a dark trail.

Remembering the metal on my tongue.

Like the taste of pennies you get… right after you pull a needle out of your arm.

Right before the rush hits you and the garden turns green.

Just when you run wild for years without ever stopping.

Until you sober up and realize everything in your garden is rotten.

SIGNED, NOT LOVED

A woman now, I find my father in the garden of this burning building.

Because he's been the only sun and one to put out the fires and rip the dirt up to till.

I lay my head in his lap.

When we're together the fire stops, the air is still.

I still wrap my grown up fingers around his rough and broken hand.

The ones who pull me from my darkness every now and then.

They're scarred and calloused from this burning building and tending to the garden.

 No matter how rough they are they feel soft every time he reaches out.

Pulls me up, helps me stand.

But I will have to do this on my own now.

I have my own garden, my own land.

It feels like I'm abandoning them when I walk away from the flames.

My back to that house and the pain that stills lives inside.

But I've built a home of my own and the garden here is flourishing.

I've got work to do so my new memories won't be the same.

I've got work to do.

Work.

Work away the pain.

Martini Monster

A monster.

I like to call it a monster because maybe that means it's not me.

Maybe if I pretend this isn't me

I can keep it up as an imposter.

The Devil talks to me more than God.

After twenty-nine days He says I should celebrate with a bottle.

But God isn't as loud, or persistent.

So the demons at my throat are what I swallow.

I call my dad. Cold on a corner in Manhattan.

There's no one else who can fight the demons with me.

He has fought them for over twenty years. A general. A winner. A soldier.

"Get in the car and go home."

I itch and scratch and grind my teeth.

"You don't have to go now, but maybe finish that cigarette and give it a think."

The longer I'm on the street the more time the Devil has a chance for us to meet.

By the time I'm halfway done smoking a martini sounds like what I need.

SIGNED, NOT LOVED

The Devil's got me by the hand and on my knees.

I can't even walk to the subway.

So many glowing bar lights beckoning me.

My soul is torn to pieces,

Every time that's all I see.

Those glowing lights.

Just for me.

But I do what they say.

I call and rely on someone else for strength.

And I may get home and I may not drink but that doesn't mean I'm safe.

With all I have at stake you would think this would be easy.

My husband. My children. My career.

You would think it would be easy.

You would think.

But these demons, I can only think about my next drink.

Thirty days tomorrow.

Thirty days of trying to figure out if I'm evil.

Or just diseased.

RACHAEL MADORI

I made it home tonight. But I still need a fix.

Just pop your Xanax and quit your shit.

At least the doctor gave that to you when your paranoia can't be released.

I've had addiction tear my life apart.

Homeless. Alone. Raped. A thief. A murderer.

And yet the glow, those neon lights that glow,

Continue to remind me that in my mind I am not alone.

They say "One day at a time."

But I don't think I'll ever be fine.

There's the Devil talking again.

In the mirror I look at Him dead in the eyes.

"You didn't get me today you fuck."

"Oh baby g\irl, I have a lifetime of more tries."

Hang on.

Dig until you can't dig no more.

Until you dig your grave.

Did You Make It?

Who knew this was feeling like you made it.

Counting pennies and saying how much you hate it.

Fell in love.

Became a wife.

Living what they call the good life.

I'll catch a plane.

Drink wine to the deepest pleasure.

I still hate people who ask about the weather.

I'll hate my past,

Enjoy my present,

Fear the future.

Truth is,

For this wound, there is no suture.

But on the real,

I'm still fake,

In so much pain.

Being real is my real disdain.

169

RACHAEL MADORI

Made in the USA
Columbia, SC
30 November 2023

f3ae48d1-c0cd-4866-a105-d1b92c52f32cR01